Latimer Briefing 11

How to Write a Theology Essay

By Michael P Jensen

The Latimer Trust

CONTENTS

How to write a theology essay

So, you've signed up for your theological studies; you've weathered the storm of those early weeks of language study (and yes, it *is* still all Greek to me); you've coped with your early forays into biblical exegesis; and you've been given a sketch of the history of the early church. There's been some spiritual highs and some frustrating lows. You can see perhaps just the beginnings of the benefits of the process of theological education creeping into your ministry – such precious minutes of it as you can grab, anyway.

But sensing a deadline looming, you go to the relevant webpage on your seminary website (past all those smiling photos of students) and discover that a strange beast is lying in wait for you: the theology essay. It might look something like this:

> *With regard to the doctrine of election, on what basis may a Christian person have personal assurance of salvation?*

or this:

> *What would be lost by denying that the resurrection of Jesus Christ from the dead was bodily?*

You have been given maybe 3,000 words in which to form an adequate response. Perhaps you are already aware of the impossibility of what is being asked, and your heart skips a beat. Whereas in, say, New Testament, there is a clear object to be studied – perhaps Paul, or John, or Colossians – here the object is *an idea.*

And the scope for answering the question is truly enormous. You have to integrate the whole teaching of Scripture with an awareness of the critical discussions that have been taking place on the matter in recent times; the two millennia of Christian thought lies on the table, running the whole gamut from Irenaeus to Miroslav Volf; you should have an awareness of philosophical challenges to the Christian view; some regard for the great creeds and confessions of the Church; and tie it all up in a tight and cogent argument.

How can anyone even begin to contemplate such a task?

That's why I wrote this book. I spend a major part of each year of my working life setting and marking theology essays. In between, I spend countless hours talking to students about how to do them. This book is a summary of many of those conversations – as well as many of the thoughts I have while I am marking the results of these chats. I should say also that what I say in this book is easily transferrable, with a few tweaks here and there, to the other sub–disciplines in a typical theology degree. I don't think teachers of church history or New Testament would dispute this.

Thanks are due to Lee Gatiss for his incisive comments; to my colleagues at Moore College, Drs Mark Thompson, David Höhne and Robert Doyle; and to my students, whom it is a delight to teach. My prayer is that students of theology will not only find their way to greater grade success, but that they will actually discover the great grace of God for them in Christ Jesus in the process.

I. How not to lose heart before you start

I recently competed in a marathon. Doesn't every middle aged man who can't afford a Porsche do this? In the months leading up to the event, it was certainly easy to say 'hey, I'm running a *marathon*' and bask in the glory of the unattempted and unachieved with that little inner smug feeling.

It was quite another to stare down the hard tarmac on a warm Sydney morning and imagine pounding it for some four hours (more like five as it turned out). Some 20 kilometres in and everything in me was saying 'you can't do this, and you should stop now'.

A theology essay can feel an awful lot like that. If you *don't* feel just a little overwhelmed, then I don't think you have really grasped the size of the mountain you are being asked to climb. As I said in my introduction, a theology essay is a complex, multi–disciplinary entity involving a conversation with ancient *and* modern texts (oh, and all the stuff in the millennia in between). Knowledge of four or five languages would help. And the history, literature and philosophy of a number of cultures. Hardest of all, it is an exercise in *thought*. It asks you to think about concepts, and to nuance them.

Making the same point, the American theologian David Bentley Hart writes:

> ...theology requires a far greater scholarly range than does any other humane science. The properly trained Christian theologian, perfectly in command of his materials, should be a proficient linguist, with a mastery of several ancient and modern tongues, should have a complete formation in the subtleties of the whole Christian dogmatic tradition, should possess a considerable knowledge of the texts and arguments produced in every period of the Church, should be a good historian, should be thoroughly trained in philosophy, ancient, medieval and modern, should have a fairly broad grasp of liturgical practice in every culture and age of the Christian world, should (ideally) possess considerable knowledge of literature, music and the plastic arts, should have an intelligent interest in the effects of theological discourse in areas such as law or economics, and so on and so

forth. This is not to say that one cannot practice theology without these attainments; but such an education remains the scholarly ideal of the guild... [1]

More of the nature of the theological task in chapters three and four – but if even a genius like Hart finds it overwhelming (and I suspect he has most of the accomplishments that he lists) then what hope have we mere hackers? What is your little effort possibly going to contribute to the discussion of centuries? How can your attempt to wrestle with the question do it justice in any way at all given the gargantuan nature of the enterprise? These theological debates have been aged in centuries like a fine whiskey is aged in oak – and we are still drinking orange squash.

But there's another thing. And it is that the task of serving Jesus and his people – which is why you signed up for theological study in the first place – seems a long way from this particular process. You aren't going to be writing essays for people who need to be shown the love of Christ and to hear the good news. The slow train of the theology essay seems to take the long way around to the destination. How is it going to help me to serve God and his people, in whatever capacity?

I am here to tell you that a) it is going to help you enormously; b) even you can do it; and c) it may even be *fun* (bear with me here).

a) the theology essay is your chance to spend serious time with your attention focused on an issue, question or problem in the knowledge of God that really matters. There is a kind of theological reasoning which is obsessed with abstract and irrelevant questions – the proverbial 'how many angels can dance on the head of a pin' question. The theologians of the Reformation period, however, insisted that theology properly done is an intensely *practical* discipline – not because it is really only concerned with what we should do, but because the knowledge of God is always relevant to the lives of men and women. There is, in fact, no more vital study than to know God and his benefits. Your

---

[1] David Bentley Hart, *In the aftermath: provocations and laments.* (Grand Rapids, Mich., William B. Eerdmans Pub. Co. 2009) p. 177

essay is going to shape you as a servant of God's people and is going to benefit you in your own spiritual life – because to know God more deeply is the goal. The Elizabethan scholar William Perkins wrote:

> Theology is the science of living blessedly for ever. Blessed life ariseth from the knowledge of God and therefore it ariseth likewise from the knowledge of ourselves, because we know God by looking into ourselves.[2]

b) ...and you can do it. Now, I haven't met you, so I don't really know at one level whether you can do it or not. But one important conviction ought to sustain you here – and that is that the knowledge of God itself is not the domain only of the clever. Let Jesus's prayer in Matthew 11:25 be your comfort: "I praise you, Father, Lord of heaven and earth, because you have hidden these things from the wise and learned, and revealed them to little children." (NIV) We are all gifted differently, and have had different educational and cultural backgrounds that make this process easy for some and less so for others. But whatever level you are at, there is a profound equality amongst Christians in terms of the knowledge of God – because this knowledge is a revealed and not a discovered knowledge. It is to that revelation of God, in Jesus Christ, that we answer in our writing of theological essays.

That's not to say that an answer full of pious observations is what is looked for in a theology essay. You aren't writing a sermon, or a devotional reflection. That's a mistake of genre that some students make. But you aren't coming at this cold – you not only know, but you are *known by* the object of your study!

c) ...and yes, it can be fun. It's overwhelming, but – what a challenge! You are being asked to think alongside some of the most profound thinkers of all history – Augustine, Aquinas, Luther. You are being invited to scale the heights and see the panoramic view at the summit – but not to do it unassisted, but alongside expert guides. You are being challenged to grow as a knower of the knowledge of

---

[2] William Perkins, *The Workes of that Famous and Worthy Minister of Christ in the Universitie of Cambridge, Mr. William Perkins*, 3 vols. (London: John Legatt, 1612-1613), I.11

God. You are being invited to hear unfamiliar voices express familiar truths. Because theological thinking emerges from the Christian gospel, which addresses all human beings everywhere and everywhen, then the discipline of theology invites you to learn from what the Holy Spirit has taught Christian believers in places that you and I can't even locate on a map.

So: what are you waiting for?

In sum:

- The topics of theology really matter
- The knowledge of God is not the preserve of the very clever
- Starting to write theology is a challenge that can be fun!

2.   What is theology in any case?

I remember my Chemistry teacher in my second year of high school very well. I remember him because he used to say things in a thick Egyptian accent like 'you late, I chop your head'.

He also said, with the all intensity of a prophet, 'chemistry – is – life'.

I was no scientist. But it was one of those exciting moments when the teacher of a certain discipline makes an impossibly grand claim for his subject to the extent that actually all the other piffling subjects on your timetable seem like excuses to fill in the days until the real business comes around. History, English, Music, Art – these were all reducible in the end to Chemistry.

Teachers of theology can often seem guilty of making this kind of exorbitant claim for their discipline over and against the other things that clutter up the timetables of the typical seminary course. But they have a great deal of difficulty explaining to students what theology actually is.

To be fair, almost any subject you can name labours under the difficulty of defining itself. If you ever want to see a fight between nerds, ask a bunch of historians or physicists what 'history' or 'physics' is. You'll have a room full of torn corduroy in no time.

But this definitional problem doesn't help you much if you are supposed to be attempting to write a piece called a 'theology essay'. And it might be matched by your own skepticism about the value of theology as a subject. Many evangelical undergraduates seem unconvinced about even the need for a thing called 'theology' in the first place. If you have a high view of the Scriptures as the Word of God, then isn't the study of the Bible the last station on the line?

We are rightly suspicious of grand theological systems that force the square pegs of Scripture into the round holes of reason. We are rightly appalled by the way in which theology can be a device for avoiding the plain meaning of the text. But these are abuses of theology – and do not describe its proper practice.

So what is it? Here's my working definition:

'Theology' is the name we give to that activity of the mind which seeks to give a coherent and intelligible articulation of the truth about God and his relation to the world, drawn from the scriptures and addressed to our contemporaries.

Notice, first, that it is a species of reason, subject to the Word of God ('coherent and intelligible...drawn from the scriptures'). That is, theology attempts to be coherent and intelligible – to make sense. It is a work of the mind, understanding that the mind is God–given and that every thought ought to be taken captive. But it is a special form of reason, which acknowledges the moral limitations of the human mind corrupted as it is by sin. As such, it follows the peculiar, distinctive and sometimes surprising shape of the Word of God; and so it is properly understood as 'exegetical reason', as Professor John Webster of Aberdeen puts it.[3]

Secondly, Christian theology is a form of speech ('...articulation of the truth'). It is a verbal form, reliant on words, the stuff of communication. Its instruments are words. While theology itself teaches us to be wary of the slipperiness of words, it also gives us heart: words are indeed capable of becoming the vehicle of God's self–communication, and the means by which we can communicate about God.

Thirdly, Christian theology has a particular subject matter: it is about God and his deeds ('the truth about God and his relation to the world'). That is, it is evangelical. The content of theology is 'merely' a reiteration – an expanded reiteration – of the gospel of the Lord Jesus Christ. Theological thinking may provide us with a point of view on any number of subjects, but it will not be true to itself if it does not relate it to the promises of God declared to mankind and fulfilled in Jesus Christ.

If it is evangelical, then, fourthly, it is also evangelistic ('about God and his relation to the world... addressed to our contemporaries'). That is to say, the purpose of Christian theology is to speak these words in the hearing of the world, inviting people near and far to submit to the Lordship of Christ Jesus. Christian theology

---

[3] John Webster, *Holy Scripture: A Dogmatic Sketch* (Cambridge: Cambridge University Press), p. 91

that is true to its task does not fold in on itself and relate itself endlessly to irresolvable speculations. Neither is it merely antiquarian: theology relates itself to today, to here and to now. Truly Christian theology serves as a call to repent and believe to which a contemporary person may respond. This has to be the case, because as Christian theology – words about the God of Christian scripture – it must share his concern for the lost and have in view his eternal purposes.

Theology – is – life.

In sum:

- Theology is a species of reason, subject to the Word of God

- Theology is a form of speech

- Theology is *evangelical:* it about God and his deeds

- Theology is *evangelistic:* it is an invitation to submit to the Lordship of Christ

3.   What is a theology essay?

Try. Have a go.

That's what an essay actually is – an attempt. The word 'essay' comes from the French word 'essayer', which means 'to try'. We owe the term to the Frenchman Michel de Montaigne who, in 1580, published a book of 'essais'. Englishman Francis Bacon turned his hand to a few 'Essayes' a couple of decades afterwards, thereby bringing the idea of the essay across the English channel.

But let's be under no illusions: the kind of thing Montaigne and Bacon wrote is not what you are being asked to write. More's the pity, too: those kinds of essays were exploratory in nature and elegant in style. It wasn't necessarily meant to persuade you of anything. Montaigne and Bacon noodled around, but it was a pleasure to watch them as they noodled. I am sorry, but if you submit a Bacon style essay you almost certainly will not do very well, though you may have more fun.

The form of the undergraduate essay in the humanities in most Western educational institutions has emerged because, in the Western way of thinking about learning, we value independence of thought and the ability to argue a case. Being asked to write an essay in the West is an invitation to state a thesis and defend a position – and to offer that as your own.

It's a notion that comes from a legal way of seeing the world, in which you get at the truth in a rather combative way – you need to take sides. That's how Western law courts work – you have lawyers who try to persuade a jury (or a judge) to believe one construction of the evidence.

Now, it is worth saying that there are of course other ways of getting at the truth – and these other ways may even be superior to the legal model. Granted. But the persuasive essay does have many benefits to it for the student. It forces you to organise your thoughts, for one. It also requires you to read deeply in one subject area. I clearly remember each of my undergraduate theology essays as landmarks in my education. Thinking is hard work, and a theology essay helps you to think.

I emphasise that it is a Western way of thinking for a reason. If you are from a non–Western background, it may be that you have become accustomed to an educational model whose emphasis is on internalising knowledge delivered by authorised instructors. However strange it may seem, the point of this exercise is to express your own informed opinion, and not someone else's. It may also be a difficult point to grasp if you have had previous tertiary training in science or engineering – disciplines in which originality of thought only gets you into trouble! But the tradition of the 'humanities' prizes the freshness of the perspective as a sign that the discipline is being internalised.

Things are not quite as straightforward as this in theology, however. Of course, in theological thinking there is a body of recognized and authoritative truths to which a writer is accountable. Theology is not the same as, say, literary criticism, in which there are no wrong answers but only bad arguments. Nevertheless, theology is one of the 'humanities' (actually, it is 'divinity', but that's another matter). It is composed of sub-disciplines like history, languages, and the interpretation of texts – all of them literary disciplines. So it makes sense to assess theology in the same way that those subjects are usually assessed.

What of originality? Well, yes, in the practice of Christian theology originality may be a vice rather than a virtue. Novelty as a principle does not bring the truth to light. I think theological essayists should reckon with this: faithfulness to the sources in front of you is as important as freshness. But it is still the case that there are many ways to express and articulate and respond to the great truths expressed in Christian orthodoxy. There may also be fresh ways to show the interconnection of these truths. So I am not willing to let go of originality as a principle so long as it is counterbalanced by a humility that says 'I must be true to the object of my study here'.

What makes a theology essay different is its purpose. The object of the theology essay is to say true things about God. Even when you are asked about something that is not God – creation, for example – the theology essay has to tell us something about God, or it is not a theology essay.

To do that it has to focus, naturally, on where God is made known to us. For evangelical theology students, that place is Holy Scripture. So, there will be a lot of Bible in a theology essay (though more about the role of Scripture in your essay later). Even so, it is important to distinguish the theology essay as a type from, say, the New Testament essay, whose goal is to tell us what the New Testament teaches. The two goals overlap of course. But whereas the New Testament essay tells us what a text says, the theology essay attempts to tell us what, when all is said and done, we may say about God himself.

To do that, the theological essayist needs to focus on concepts. Ideas. Thoughts. They are funny things, ideas: they aren't objects in the world like chairs and tables and laboratory rats. And they aren't events that can be accessed through witnesses. (Now theology in fact involves objects and events as it turns out – but it is primarily the thinking about them as ideas and in terms of the ideas that spring from them that involves you, the would-be essayist. But more of that later).

But it is more than just 'ideas' that are your concern. You are being asked to order ideas, in the form of an argument. How are the ideas connected? How do they relate? What do they amount to in the end? What are the implications of this connection of concepts?

That's why it is important for the student to realise that the theological essay does not merely summarise the teaching of scripture on a given subject. It is not a Bible dictionary article. It does that summative task, sure: but it does more. That's what makes it a challenge. One of the things that theological essayists have to reckon with is that their chief source, Scripture, is composed of a variety of different types of literature only some of which look at all like the piece of writing they are attempting to compose themselves. And Scripture doesn't explicitly answer all the theological questions that might be asked of her.

The theology essay will hopefully distil, synthesize and extrapolate the teaching of Scripture. It will distil it in that it will articulate what the whole of Scripture teaches with as much clarity as possible. It will synthesize in that it will look at the diversity of Scripture and try to find its points of coherence. It will extrapolate in that it will make explicit what is merely implicit in the Bible, or make connections where the connections have not been articulated.

So, remember: a theology essay is an invitation to express an argument of your own. It's about God. And it will contain ideas.

In sum

- An essay is an invitation to persuade
- The object of the theology essay is to say true things about God
- The theology essay deals with ideas and concepts
- It is not merely a summary of Scripture

4. The responsibility of theology

You may be impatient to get on with it now. After all, there's a deadline looming, and lots to do.

But I want to slow it down a little and ask you to consider something vital about the whole nature of this piece of attempted thinking in which you are about to engage. Theology is a unique science because it has as its object the holy God himself. That means that, even though the theology essay is an academic exercise, it is not by any means a merely academic exercise.

It's God we are dealing with here. 'Take off your shoes', we might say. 'You are walking on holy ground'.

The object of this study dwells in unapproachable light. 'Our God is a consuming fire', and is not a creature whose biorhythms and mating habits we might study. And our God has spoken, in the past by the prophets, and finally and decisively in the person of his Son, who is the exact imprint of his being.

How could we hope to say anything that isn't a blasphemy? How could we hope to say anything that isn't, at least potentially, the making of an idol?

And yet, the guts of the matter is that a word has been spoken; and that God has invited human beings to repeat and explain and explore this word, to 'take every thought captive' in his service.

What this means for theology – and for your theology essay – is that it must be humble before its object and responsible to it. If any verse is to be the theologian's motto it is 'the fear of the Lord is the beginning of wisdom'. If you do not fear the Lord, then what, may I ask, are you doing studying theology? There are theology students who have embarked on the study of theology as a matter of mere interest, perhaps because they are struck by the breadth of the intellectual challenge before them. They may be fascinated by theology, even devoted to it. But if they are not devoted to God, then theology has itself become a false god. An interest in theology for its own sake is a perversion of the true end of theology – which is not just to know about God, but to know him and make him known.

And that means being responsible – in the sense of answerable – to it. The Lord whom we are called to fear is the judge of all. There is no trifling with this God! And he has spoken. Whatever thoughts we may have are after the fact of this speech. The criterion for successful theology is quite simply 'is it faithful to God's own revelation of himself?' For you that means that you ought to have no truck with playing intellectual games in your essay. You have no business simply showing off your intellectual brilliance. One of the worst temptations of the theological student is the temptation to innovate for its own sake – to revel in the high of sublime ideas for their own sake. I confess that this is sometimes my own temptation: ideas are delightful, the life of the mind scintillating and the consequences truly dreadful.

Can a bad person do good theology? I was once in a master's seminar with Professor Oliver O'Donovan where he posed this question. Of course, the answer is 'I really hope so' because there are no other kinds of human person. But O'Donovan had in mind as 'bad' the person who really had no fear of God at all, and who showed in his or her life only disregard and even contempt for God. He confessed that he had encountered such people – and, I regret to say, so have I. They may do brilliant intellectual work. But it is not good theology.

Those who write theology are not only limited creatures, but are sinful, and they stand before a holy God. And that is why they must start their work with prayer. They really have no other option. They must ask for God's help – they must start with this humble act, and submit their intellects to his service.

Here's what they might pray:

Father of all wisdom, I praise you that in your Son Jesus Christ you have made yourself known to men and women: enlighten and guide me by your Holy Spirit as I begin this work; help me in my weakness to think truly about you and in my pride to be humble before you; keep me from falsehood, and make me your servant in the building of your church; in the name of your Son by whose death and resurrection we have new life to the praise of your glorious grace: Amen.

And that prayer includes a final thought: that theology that begins with prayer will be done in the service of God and his people. There ought to be nothing self-indulgent about theological study. I trust you have begun your course of study in theology because you want to serve God's people, in whatever way. Your study will no doubt be of enormous spiritual benefit to you. But it will, I pray, be of enormous benefit to the church, too.

Does that make a difference to your approach to your theology essay? I most certainly hope it does. Not because anyone other than the marker will ever read it necessarily! But because this essay is an opportunity to know God better so that you might make him known more truly. It doesn't mean you will choose the most 'relevant' topic, or the most contentious, or the most obviously pastoral. It doesn't mean you will 'dumb down' your answer. The opposite in fact: you should be motivated to do as thorough a job as possible, because you are seeking to serve God and his people – humble before him, responsible to his revelation of himself, and seeking the benefit of others in what you do.

POSTSCRIPT

Because of its object – God – theology makes particular demands on its students. But in making these demands, it actually can teach other fields of study about how they should go about their work. There is an ethics, or a spirituality of theological study. And so there ought to be with any subject. The kind of faithfulness to its object that theology requires ought to be present in every field. Just as theology treats its object as holy and seeks to known it on its own terms – God as he reveals himself – there is a sense in which any discipline ought to revere its object and seek to serve it. The worst kind of academic work is found when the things that are studied become merely the tools in some kind of intellectual game. This certainly happened somewhat in the field of literary studies, in which I received my early training. The great literary works disappeared from university courses and were replaced by a plethora of options for study including an emphasis on literary theory.

I am not against literary theory. But to study it as a study in and of itself seems to perpetuate a circle of self-indulgence – and to prove that much of it is not designed to say anything about literary texts, but rather to focus our attention elsewhere. You can't know something properly without in some way humbling yourself before it. This is as true for physics or history as it is for theology.

In sum:

- Theology is answerable to God and must be done with prayerful reverence

- Theology is best done in service to God and his people

5.   Choosing the question

The common practice of colleges is to provide a list of questions –
perhaps six or so – from which the students may choose. Doubtless
they do this to stop the markers dying of boredom and to make sure
that library resources are evenly spread amongst students. Good
reasons, perhaps: but it adds a layer of decision-making to the whole
process which may cause you some stress – especially if you are one
of those people who can never decide what colour socks to wear in the
morning.

And the truth of the matter is that this is one of those
decisions you are going to make that you have to make without fully
knowing what it will look like at the end of the process. It's a bit like
getting married: you have to sort of guess on the basis of the
piecemeal information you have what is going to work out best. And
there's years to regret the decision if it is made poorly. (Of course, the
analogy breaks down in several obvious ways. There's no party when
you choose your essay topic. Your friends won't give you presents.
And... OK, maybe it was a rubbish analogy to begin with.)

But still: you are going to spend (well I hope!) a lot of hours
wedded to this question – and not to some other possibly very
interesting and worthwhile questions – so the decision is worth
taking carefully.

Cast your eye over the list of essay questions. What
immediately interests you? Usually, you will get a quick sense of what
topic area a question is addressing, and you may have a sense already
of a topic area that interests you. Perhaps a particular topic has been
smouldering away in your mind for a while. Or perhaps you can
immediately see how an issue will have benefits for your ministry. It
might be that several of the questions have this effect. Asterisk them.

But it is worth looking a little more closely. It could be that
the topic is of interest to you, but that the question is angled in a
particular way so as to take it out of your frame of interest. I often
speak with students who say, a couple of weeks in to the assignment,
'I thought the essay was a question that was going to help me resolve
x, but actually it has drawn me to y.' Or, worse: I have marked essays
that have been addressed to a vague topic area, say 'the doctrine of

election', but not to the specific question about the doctrine of election, say 'in what sense is Christ 'the mirror of our election?' (John Calvin). We'll talk about analysing the question later; but it is worth noting that a topic and a question are somewhat different beasts and need to be held in separate cages in the zoo of your mind. Or they'll fight, honest.

Now, a couple more things are worth taking into account here. Many students will ask themselves quite straightforwardly 'which essay is the easiest'? This is entirely understandable, especially if you have a low opinion of yourself as a student, or if you are not used to essay writing. But beware: the question that seems easiest may not be at all. Most students are attracted to a more general question – the kind of question that is asked in familiar terms and which appears to allow you scope to repeat information you already know or at least have a hunch you might know where to find. Here's an example of such a question:

Discuss the doctrine of justification by faith alone.

This seems like a real 'gimme putt', to use a golfing term; or an open goal, in football terms. Once when I was in primary school, in my only game as a striker for the senior football team, the ball popped over the defenders' heads, leaving me in the clear bearing down on an open goal with the keeper out of his area. I vividly remember stabbing at the ball with my toe and watching it veer off wildly in the direction of the corner flag. I also remember the guffaws of the opposing team.

This could happen with this apparently easy essay. Why? Because it is vague. It looks like all you have to do is really simple. But it is actually asking you to do all the work in framing a response. 'Discuss' is a word that should alarm you – because it could mean almost anything. There is no frame of reference given in the question. It is actually a badly asked question in educational terms – but your teachers are fallible and you see this sort often enough, alas. The vagueness of the question will lead to the vagueness of your answer unless you are very careful.

So: don't just try to choose the easiest. Usually that is impossible to tell, and the easiest-looking one usually isn't. And it is a wasted opportunity to stretch yourself, too.

My advice would also be not to choose a topic because it is an opportunity to address a current church controversy – women's ministry, or charismatic gifts, for example. It is good to think about these questions, of course! But inevitably, as a marker I find that these essays are skewed by feelings and polemics and tend to fall short of the mark as pieces of academic theological thinking. In the end, giving your time and your mind to an issue more at the heart of the theological enterprise is likely to equip you better to respond to controversy in any case.

It is worth getting a sense for what your class mates might be doing. I am tempted to feed your cynicism here and say this is because it is easier to stand out in a smaller crowd – so choose the question that no-one else appears to be doing because you'll get a better mark. But there two good reasons to consider what others are doing. First, it may be that library resources are limited and that you'll do everyone a favour by attempting the question that is standing by looking desperate and dateless. Second, it's because there could be a good chance for some collaborative learning and there are people who are doing this question who'd you like to work with. I'll say some more about working with other students a bit later – it's a practice which has obvious advantages but some hidden disadvantages.

But above all: go with something that interests you. It could be that you are intrigued and can't imagine yet what an answer might be. It could be that you are going to have an opportunity to read the work of a great theologian whose work you haven't read before. It could be that you already have a sense of what the answer might be and you're itching to put it down on paper. If none of the questions interests you, I don't know what to suggest – but why are you studying theology?!

POSTSCRIPT

In some circumstances you may be invited to make up your own question. It might be a final year project, or a later-year course in which a general topic area is given. For some students this is the worst thing in the world – it brings out all their vices of indecision. They can never settle on a topic or on a question within that topic. If this is you: I don't know quite what to suggest except for you to make a decision and stick with it!!! I can't help you more than that really!

But the trick here is to narrow it down. You aren't writing a PhD. Most students are far too ambitious in what they propose. If you have a big question you are intent on answering, see yourself as just taking a slice off the top of it rather than doing the whole thing. Focus is what you want – you need to make space for yourself to mount a plausible argument and to marshal the necessary evidence. So for example: 'Evaluate the traditional doctrine of original sin' would make a great book. It is possible to write something pretty good in a few thousand words on this. But why not make it: 'Evaluate Augustine's doctrine of original sin?' This gets you to focus on a particular set of texts rather than a potentially enormous array of materials.

In sum:

- Choose a topic that interests you, but look carefully at the question

- Avoid a topic that is a contemporary church controversy where possible

- Consider what others are doing

6.   Analysing the question

Right. Prayers said, question chosen. What now?

Your mind has already started ticking about the question and perhaps some ideas have started running around in your head in no particular organised fashion. This is not bad, this chaos. One of the things you have to realise with this thinking work you're are doing is that your brain is an organism and is organised like an organism, not like something designed by Steve Jobs, made in China and sold for an incredible mark-up. You have to coax it into working for you. But it will work for you in unexpected ways and at times that you won't be ready for it and necessarily conscious of what is happening (or even, actually, conscious at all. That's why we say 'sleep on it'.)

But you do need to look more closely at the actual question and ask what it is really about. We all know what a crime it is to not answer the question. So it is good to figure out what the question is actually asking you to do, so that you do that and not some other thing.

Here's the first thing to look for: the verb. What is it asking you to do? And here I'll let you into a little secret. A while ago – 1956 it was – a man named Benjamin Bloom thought far too hard about this sort of thing and came up with 'Bloom's taxonomy' of educational goals. That is: he listed a whole bunch of skills that educators like to get students to show they have: knowledge, comprehension, application, analysis, synthesis and evaluation. All of these are important, but the scale increases in complexity from knowledge through to evaluation. And it is the last three of these that educators in tertiary education are especially interested in assessing.

So, your research essay will most often be couched in terms of (if not in the words of) analysis, synthesis and evaluation. These are the skills that you are supposed to be showing. Sure, you will need to know stuff, and understand it. But you need to pay attention to where the question is asking you to attend to one of these higher order skills.

But there's a trap. Sometimes a question doesn't explicitly ask you to do one of these things. Never mind: *do them anyway*. Shape the question to fit these goals. Be sure that you will be assessed according to how well you did them, whether the question directly asks you to or not. Believe me here.

Take this question for example:

Evaluate the arguments for and against universalism, with special reference to the work of Jurgen Moltmann.

This is pretty straightforward: the verb is evaluate. What does that mean? It means weigh up; give a value to. Make a judgement. How good are the arguments on both sides?

But what about this question:

What is the nature and extent of progress in the Christian life?

Now you can immediately see that there is no verb asking you to do anything at all here. But you still need to ask: what is the question asking me to evaluate/synthesise/analyse? Where is my judgement being called for? In this instance, the question is asking you to analyse the concept of progress in the Christian life and then make an informed judgement as to extent. That's going to take some synthesising and evaluating, isn't it?

Another way of analyzing the question is to find the 'question' word – is it a 'why', a 'how', 'what', 'when' or even 'who'? The first three deserve some reflection. Why questions are asking you to locate a cause or purpose. Thus the classic essay question –

Why did God become man?

– asks you to trace both the causes and the purpose of the incarnation of the Son of God (and you need to talk to Athanasias and Anselm by the way!).

'What' questions appear to be asking you to describe something:

What is the impact of Arianism for Christian teaching about salvation?

The danger here is that you will just tell me something and not show it to me. Remember, you are being asked to display the higher level skills on Dr Bloom's chart. Summary and description aren't enough.

How questions are asking you to talk about the way in which something is done – to examine the inner workings of an event or an argument. The event or argument is often a 'given' of the question. Take this for example:

> *How is it that all human beings may be said to share in the sin of Adam?*

You are encouraged to assume that all humans do share in Adam's sin, and to explain how this is. You could challenge the presupposition of the question of course, but that's a high-risk strategy.

The next thing you need to figure out is the reference point or context against which you are supposed to make your evaluation. Once again, this can be quite explicitly stated, or it may be that you have to infer it from the question yourself. Either way, you need a yardstick against which you are going to judge the issue. What are your criteria, in other words?

Take our first sample question:

> *Evaluate the arguments for and against universalism, with special reference to the work of Jürgen Moltmann.*

Forget Jürgen Moltmann for a moment. You have been asked to evaluate two opposing sides to a question – that of universalism. But according to... what criteria? The question doesn't say, so you are going to have to supply the criteria. But you can assume that, in theology, the usual criteria is faithfulness to Scripture and to the norms of good theological thinking that your institution or college have set forward. Is it biblical? Is it orthodox? Is it coherent? These would be important reference points to keep in mind. But also, it is a comparative question, asking for you to lay two alternatives side by side.

Here's another question:

> *Is 'conscious eternal torment' the only sound biblical and theological description of the nature of hell?*

In this instance there are given reference points against which you are to evaluate the particular position – the Bible, and 'theology'. Note that in this instance, you aren't being asked to come with a new argument as much as to evaluate a pre-existing one.

Now what about this one:

To what extent did the Eternal Son 'empty himself' of his divine nature when he came to earth?

'To what extent' gives you a evaluative action to do: how far does this proposal run, as you see it? But what's the reference point here? By what standard are you going to measure the 'extent'? It may be that you are going to have to articulate the reference point in your answer.

One thing's worth adding here. It's a theology essay in the context of a course called 'Doctrine' or 'Theology'. The questions make sense when seen in the history and practice of this discipline. For example the scare quotes in the 'conscious eternal torment' question are there because this is language that has been used in a debate going back some centuries. You are being invited to join this debate. Likewise, when mention is made of 'the doctrine of justification', the assumption is that there is such a thing available to analyse and debate. And there is – in the history of Christian thought. Or, a specific thinker might be named – such as 'Jurgen Moltmann'. That's a pretty obvious way of reminding you that you are engaging in a conversation that has been going on a long while already. So what you need to do is to locate your question in the context of the theological conversation that is already there. (I'll talk a bit more about joining the conversation later on.)

Having asked yourself what you are being asked to do, it is now time to look at the specific content of the question. You'll quickly observe that essay questions take all kinds of forms:

a) *Evaluate Calvin's claim that "Wherever we see the Word of God purely preached and heard, and the sacraments administered according to Christ's institution, there, it is not to be doubted, a church of God exists."*

b) *Is there any sense in which we can say that 'the world is charg'd with the grandeur of God?' (G.M. Hopkins). Answer with regard to the doctrine of revelation.*

c) *With regard to the doctrine of the Holy Spirit, and in the light of the effect of sin on human understanding, in what sense (if any) can it be said that Scripture is clear?*

The questions are padded out in a variety of ways. Often a quotation is added to the question. You have to decide whether the quotation is an integral part of the question or whether it is just there for aesthetic purposes. In question a) above, the quote from Calvin is the very thing you are supposed to be evaluating. Note, too, that it is specifically labelled as Calvin's claim: that is, you are being invited not only to engage with the proposition on its own terms but as a claim made by the theologian John Calvin, as part of his thought. You'd be right to try and locate the quotation in context and to engage with Calvin's thought more broadly (though the question is not asking for a history lesson, but an analysis, don't forget).

But question b) uses a quote from the Jesuit poet Gerard Manley Hopkins. And very nice it is too. But the question itself gives you enough indications that you are not supposed to give an analysis of Hopkins' thought, fascinating though that would be. In fact, you can answer the question without ever having heard of Hopkins.

Question c) offers you a specific frame of reference for your analysis of the proposition 'Scripture is clear'. The markers want to help you by pointing you to the doctrine of the Holy Spirit and the effects of sin on human knowing. The question could have stood alone in the form –

In what sense (if any) can it be said that Scripture is clear?

But you have been given specific directives as to the shape of your answer here. You can't avoid them.

What about this monster:

'The church will stay on mission as it reflects deeply on the sacraments as gospel dramas where the Word is spoken and made visible, and where the blessings of life with the triune God brought to us through the Word made flesh, who died for our sin and rose for our new life, are lived out faithfully in the sacramental community of the Spirit to the glory of God the Father.'

How may we adequately conceive of the nature and role of sacraments in ecclesiology?

These questions, in my experience, drive students absolutely batty. You have a long and complicated – and unnamed – quotation which is placed above a question with no given connection to it. What are you to do with the quotation?

Students will overcomplicate things at this stage and try and locate the quotation and interact specifically with it. But there is no directive in the question that asks you to do anything. The best thing to do is to see the quotation as a piece of stimulus material. The question itself is what should absorb your attention. The quotation (I would make reference to it, or incorporate some mention of it just to be sure) is not the main business.

Lastly, it is worth considering whether the question is a 'leading question'. Is the questioner trying to lead you in a particular direction with the way the question is asked? I hate to say it, but it is one of the foibles of question-askers that they do it. It is good to be a bit suspicious of this as you analyse the question – is there a presumed 'right' answer given what you know about the institution and the predilections of your teachers? I say this not so you can trot out the politically correct answer of course, but so that you can show that you are making a fair assessment of all the evidence in the right context.

In sum:

- What higher level task am I being asked to do, explicitly or implicitly?

- Am I being asked to find a cause or a purpose, or trace a connection, or describe something?

- What is the measure I am being asked to use, explicitly or implicitly?

- Where is my question located in the context of the ongoing theological conversation?

- Are there any extra features of the question that I have to take into account?

7. Beginning to think about it

Thinking is actually hard work.

Now it doesn't look like it is, because you do a lot of it sitting down, and you don't sweat much doing it. You don't get callouses anywhere, and you don't put your back out for the most part.

But it is hard. Done properly, thinking is exhausting. That's why we watch TV – because it is like we are having someone else do our thinking for us.

Why am I telling you this? Because you need to treat your brain well if you are going to get the most out if it for your essay. It is like any other part of your body, and needs to be rested and exercised for it to operate at its best. And sometimes, in order to get our brain going, we use that extra kick of stress that an approaching deadline brings. It focuses our attention on a task and we switch into action mode.

There's a whole theology essay to be written about the way in which we have thought of our 'minds' as somehow separate from our bodies and expected them to work as something machine-like, and how we forget that our minds are affected by tiredness, depression, age, lack of sleep, caffeine and boredom just as our bodies are. But I won't give you that here. Suffice it to say: your mind is a part of your body and you need to cultivate it as you cultivate your body to get the most out of it.

Let me plead with you here. If you are addicted to using adrenaline to get your tasks done and your deadlines met, could you consider weaning yourself off it? Trouble is, you may have done perfectly well throughout your academic career till now by getting that buzz and watching your fingers burn up the keyboard. You stoke up the espresso machine, sit down at your desk and go from zero to three thousand in a few hours. When I was an undergraduate doing an English degree, a friend of mine used to say that it wasn't a proper essay until you had sprinted across the campus to the faculty office at 4:55pm (essays were due at 5:00pm) with the essay in your hand flapping in the breeze.

But the results won't be what they could be. And you won't teach yourself to think at depth. You won't allow your thinking to reach a maturity that this subject – the knowledge of God – deserves. And – let me be even more guilt-inducing, at least for those who are studying theology for the ministry – it isn't what the people of God deserve from you either. You might be good at winging it, but (speaking as a winger of it from way back) it won't be nearly as good as you could produce otherwise.

So the point is this: get your brain whirring on this topic as soon as you possibly can. An hour spent on the essay eight weeks out from the deadline will be worth three hours the week before. My experience is that the subconscious part of your brain will work in the background for you. And you will be alerted to pick up references, thoughts and ideas as you go around doing other things, too. (Which is why I find quantifying time spent on an assignment almost completely meaningless – do I count the ten minutes I spent thinking about it while I was having a shower, or on hold to the help desk in Bangalore?)

In the process of thinking about a project, time off not thinking about it can be as productive as time on. So (and this should be true for you in your whole programme of education) do not neglect holidays or weekends or talking to your spouse. Don't give up exercise. Start exercising if you haven't already. The best thing for your essay may be consistent exercise, because it will clear your mind and reduce that flustered feeling stress brings.

So that's why I advise choosing your question as early as possible and then spending an hour brainstorming almost immediately.

And how should you begin to do that? Once you have analysed the question and decided what it is that you are being asked to do, there are two vital next steps. The first of these is to ask 'what kind of response to the question might I give here?' The second is 'do I need to clarify or define any part of the question so I don't go wrong?'

The first thing to do is to imagine what possible ways of responding there might be. This is a hypothetical exercise because as yet you won't be sure of the answer to the question, naturally. You may have some inklings – fine. Note them down. But the vital thing is to turn the question into a potential thesis statement, or line of argument.

You should do this by doing what our English teachers used to tell us when we were doing 'comprehension' exercises. Now I hated these, but teachers always wanted us to use 'full sentence answers' – by which they meant, turn the question into a statement with an answer in it. Here's an example:

How is it that all human beings may be said to share in the sin of Adam?

You should write something like: 'All human beings may be said to share in the sin of Adam because ... ' and then try to complete the sentence. Does anything come to mind? Can you think of some possibilities? 'All human beings share in the sin of Adam because'... hmm...what about.. 'they all share his genetic inheritance'? It doesn't matter at this stage if you haven't got much to say, but the exercise forces you to recognise what kind of thing you are looking for.

And your suggested, sketched out answer will perhaps suggest the need for some further thought and clarification of the ideas. How do we know about this? What alternative proposals immediately spring to mind?

And this leads to the second step. And this is where you need to do some preliminary quick reading and compile some possible avenues of inquiry, just to orient yourself. At this stage, theology dictionary articles, Wikipedia and even plain old Google are your friend. Remember, this is just getting your head in the right place for now, not detailed research.

Wikipedia, did I hear you say? But we've been told not to use Wikipedia! Quite right, too. Don't use Wikipedia in your actual reading on a topic. But Wikipedia is a remarkable and quick source for the basic facts you will need to orient yourself to a topic and clear up any misunderstandings or bewilderments. I have spoken with professional journalists who use Wikipedia to orient themselves in this way without ever making it their definitive source. Who is Jürgen Moltmann? What is 'providence'? What was Arianism?

Right. What you need to do now is find a blank piece of paper or a whiteboard and simply brainstorm.

About which more in the next chapter.

In sum:

- Get your brain moving early on
- What different ways of answering the question are there?
- Do some preliminary quick reading to orient yourself to the topic

8.   Brainstorming

If you are in possession of a brain and faced with the task of completing a theology essay, brainstorming is an indispensable activity and you'd better get into it. (Someone told me recently that 'brainstorming' is now not a politically correct term, and that we all have to have 'thought showers', in case the epileptic community is offended. You can't make this stuff up!)

Having determined what the question actually means, the aim of your initial brainstorm is to get down on paper everything you can think of in no particular order.

Remember: thinking is a physical activity. At this point I personally need to use pen and paper, or a whiteboard. (If I use a whiteboard, I then take a digital photo and upload it for later). I can't really explain why, but using the old-style messy handwriting just works to unlock the sleepy bits of my brain.

What are you looking for? Well what I end up with isn't pretty. It's a sketch with lots of question marks, and lines going all over the place as I trace out possible connections between thoughts. I haven't read much yet, so I just don't know what I am going to find. I guess I am listing a series of doors to open, without knowing what doors are going to lead into passageways, and further doors, and even whole rooms, and what doors are going lead nowhere.

What I am looking for is possibilities. Ideas to follow and things to read. So: here is a good place to make a preliminary list of scriptural passages that are going to be obvious touchstones for you. If you know already of any obvious conversation partners in the history of theology, jot them down here too.

Just say the question is this:

What would be lost by denying that the resurrection of Jesus Christ from the dead was bodily?

Now, analysing the question I have come up with the sub-question 'lost from what'? – and I have recognised that the question is asking me to make a defence of the traditional understanding of the resurrection of Jesus Christ as bodily. There's a negative in place here – how would a non-bodily resurrection be deficient?

Well I am obviously going to have to hunt around for some thinkers who might argue that the resurrection of Jesus Christ from the dead wasn't a bodily resurrection. Now, I have heard it said that Bishop John Shelby Spong argues against this so I jot his name down. That doesn't mean he is going to feature in my essay – far from it: he's not a scholarly source, he's a 'popular' author – but looking at his books might at least alert me to other places to look. I have also heard something about Anglican Archbishop of Perth Peter Carnley, so I'll jot his name down.

Clearly this isn't a very long list, so I had better commit to further investigation of the other side of the case. If my portrayal of the case against the bodily resurrection is deficient then my argument in defence of it will also be weak. So I must be careful to find the strongest opponent to argue with. (more of that later).

What could possibly be the opposite case? A resurrection that is spiritual only? No resurrection at all? It is important to consider the alternatives and how someone could possibly argue for them.

Can I think at this stage of any possibilities of things that might be lost? A couple of possibilities come to mind, because I think of the bodily resurrection in terms of the strong affirmation of the body and of the created order in the New Testament. In fact, Romans 8 is a very interesting passage in this regard and says something about the 'redemption of our bodies'. That'll be worth a further look.

Also, the resurrection of Jesus as a body is something that then gets used as an image to talk about the church, which is 'his body'. I don't quite know what to make of that, but – well, it's worth scratching it down for now.

What about the Bible? Romans 8 I've already mentioned. 1 Corinthians 15 is going to be the obvious place to look and I am going to have to do some exegetical work in and around that passage. But where else? The Old Testament? Ezekiel 37 and Daniel 12 are the standard resurrection passages. But also, later Isaiah talks a lot about the new creation – maybe that's worth a look. Psalm 16? The preaching in Acts? Note it down. We can add to this list later.

Now whatever you do: don't lose this sketch of paper! File carefully! This work will be your reference in the weeks to come.

In sum:

- Get everything you can think of down on paper in no particular order

- What thinkers might be relevant? Especially look for potential opponents

- What passages of Scripture might be worth investigating?

9. How to read for theology essays (and what to read)

The theology essay is in many respects an exercise in reading. It is measuring how well and how widely you can read in the area of the question.

Because theology is an invitation to engage in a discussion that has been developing for two millennia, it would be arrogant AND daft to ignore the work of people who have gone before you. Now this can sound a little intimidating – there's so much to read! And what can I possibly say that hasn't been said already? Part of me wants to say 'good – be intimidated!' If you haven't grasped this, you are flirting with danger. But I would also want to say that entering this conversation gives you the benefit of all those who have gone before you. You can 'stand on the shoulders of giants' as they say, and see just a little bit further than them perhaps.

The thing here is not to get swamped – especially in your first round of reading. The idea of this first lot of reading is to get into the topic and see what it looks like – to get your bearings.

Visiting a new city is a bit like this. I visited Skopje in Macedonia recently, and I decided to go for a run early in the morning. I was afraid of getting lost amongst the blocks of 1960s flats. But Skopje has very visible orientation points: the river Vardar that courses through the city; a large mountain range on one side, with a 64 metre cross on its crown; and a city centre out from which the main roads radiate. In the end it was fairly simple, once these great landmarks had been located. 'Keep the river on your right and the mountain on your left' I said to myself as I sweated my way home. (I got a few strange looks from the locals, too: I don't think early morning exercise is what Skopjans do.)

That's what you are trying to locate in the question you are attempting: what are the great mountains and rivers in the discussion that will help you find where you are? Who are the great thinkers? What are the great issues that have arisen?

Your focus in the first instance should be broad. You should be reading quickly – for sketch information, not detail. You want to maximise your efforts by reading intensively in the things most worth reading – not getting bogged down on day one in irrelevant material. If you start reading something and it isn't what you need, move on.

Preliminary investigations should take you to one or more of the dictionaries of theology that are available. I use the New Dictionary of Theology (IVP), for example. Inevitably, the articles in these dictionaries have bibliographies which will give you a sense of what is most worth reading in this area. This is an important tip for research as a matter of fact: check the bibliographies of the things you are reading for further items to read.

But I also have in mind that I will check what some of the true greats in the tradition of Christian thought have said on a particular subject – almost no matter what subject that is. Augustine, for example, is such an important figure for all subsequent theology in the West – and he usually has something relevant to say. The Cappadocian Fathers are also worth visiting on many topics. As a Protestant, I am always interested in what Calvin and Luther had to say in the 16th century. In the middle ages, Thomas Aquinas is the mightiest figure. I am also interested in picking up from the seventeenth century the way in which the Protestant tradition systematised their thinking in the work of people like Francois Turretin. Moving forward, it is worth checking Friedrich Schleiermacher, the Father of modern liberalism – even if just to disagree with him. Then in the twentieth century, I always check Karl Barth, Wolfhart Pannenberg, Jürgen Moltmann and more conservative figures like Herman Bavinck and the recent work of Reformed thinkers like say, Gerald Bray[4] and Kevin Vanhoozer.

The amount of reading that you will have to do will of course vary depending on what level of study you are attempting. On the whole, the emphasis on secondary reading will increase the further on you go in your studies.

Each of these writers are well indexed – and that's crucial. Use indexes to minimise the amount of irrelevant reading you have to do. Pinpoint exactly the right spot, and quickly get a sense of what is being said. Make short notes, file them carefully and move on.

---

[4] See in particular Gerald Bray's book *God is Love – A Biblical and Systematic Theology* (Wheaton, Illinois: Crossway, 2012)

Oh, and just a point about working on your computer. In these early stages, as you read, it is tempting to cut and paste into a word file chunks of material that you are reading – and very easy to forget to attribute it. Then, as you come to write up your essay, you forget that that chunk of writing actually was written by someone else, and just paste it into your essay unattributed. It's an easy mistake to make, but careful note taking will remedy it as you go. Plagiarism is not an ancient church heresy found by Plagiarius: it is a sin taken quite seriously by contemporary colleges and universities. Even if it is accidental, you are still responsible for your work.

What else should you read? Don't forget to take notice of the electronic resources available to you for quick and accurate searches of recent journal articles. You should scan journals like *The Scottish Journal of Theology* and *Modern Theology* for articles relevant to your subject. The thing about journal articles, however, is that they tend to be highly focussed, highly specialised pieces of writing. That is their great benefit and their great flaw (for you and your essay). The highly focussed nature of the journal article means that it can get the point more quickly than a larger work. But you may find that an article that comes up when you search for articles on 'resurrection' is entitled 'Hans Urs von Balthasar's view of the resurrection in his Theological Aesthetics, in conversation with Hans Küng'. That is possibly interesting (really!), but too specialised for your purposes here. Take note, however, of names of authors you might have read before – an article by contemporary theologian Miroslav Volf, for example, will be part of his much larger body of work on a subject and might be worth chasing through.

It is worth asking: what am I reading for? What am I seeking to gain from this reading?

First, you are reading to gain basic information. The reading should give you simply more things to say – a wider grasp of the details on view and the particulars of the subject. Recently, I marked a paper which was a coherent and lucid essay, and actually answered the question in its own way (so I reluctantly passed it). But because the student, who only listed three bibliographical items, had clearly not read very much at all, he (or she) had completely missed the very vigorous debate that had occurred about the subject. Reading would have given him the basic information that he needed for a proper answer.

Second, you are reading for the purpose of deepening your understanding of what is involved in the question. You are reading to complexify things – to gain nuance and subtlety. Where has this question taken other thinkers? That is why it is a complete must to read the works of the big fish and not the minnows. You won't get complexity and depth if you hang out with minor minds.

Actually, that's really vital, so I'll say it again: swim with the big fish, don't paddle with the minnows. You can trail in the wake of some big fish: the standard of your work will increase because you are riding on their strength. One of my pet hates is reading a theology essay that refers only to the works of popular preachers. Do these guys do good theology? Sometimes. But it is usually derivative and simplified. That's why they are good at being popular preachers – they make things simple! Read them for your devotions, but keep them out of your essay! (Let me be clear: I don't want to see the names Keller, Driscoll or Mahaney in an essay ever again! Fair enough? What about Stott, or Piper? Well be careful – they have both written scholarly works, but more often they are 'popular'. Learn to distinguish).

Third, you are reading to develop arguments you can use. Remember, you are trying to form a thesis statement, or an argument. Mine the theologians for arguments that seem persuasive. Is their synthesis of Scripture viable, as far as you are concerned? Is it worth taking some of that wisdom on board? Modify if you need to.

Fourth, you are reading to find stimulating conversation partners. We read because the people we hang out with usually are those who agree with us. They come from where we come from. When we read, we are able to have access to the meditations and expositions of people from another time and place – and they may have perspectives on the subject that we would never be able to see. You don't have to agree with everything they say, but they may push you to discover a great deal about your own position, or to develop a new position that takes into account things they have said.

One of my teachers used to talk about finding 'surprising friends'. What he meant was: when you find someone from a perspective that is completely alien to yours with whom you can actually agree, this adds quite a deal of weight to your argument. You can't just be dismissed as a product of your own context if someone with vastly different presuppositions comes to similar conclusions.

Fifth, you are reading to find out what the opposition says! You are reading because you need to read first hand the best case you can find against the position you want to run. For example: you need to know what those who deny the bodily resurrection are saying before you can argue properly against them in defence of the bodily resurrection. Otherwise your essay will descend to mere polemics.

That is: you aren't reading to find the craziest, most extreme point of view on the topic. You are reading to find what the most serious and sophisticated and convincing theological arguments are. You need to be brave to do this, I know. I used to have the habit of finding the most nutty scholar I could find, and then writing an essay in response to them. My 'surprising friends' teacher read one of my pieces like this and said 'well, what have you achieved? Your opponent is simply wrong! You didn't need to tell me this! There is no credit to you if you defeat them'.

It would be like sending off Manchester United to play against the Lewisham under 10s. Does it prove that Man U are the best team in the world when they beat the under 10s 42 – 0? No, it doesn't – with no disrespect to the boys from Lewisham. A real test is when they play Barcelona: that would actually prove something.

You have to locate your Barcelonas, and Chelseas, and AC Milan. Beat them, and then you'll have something to brag about.

In sum:

- Read to gain basic information

- Read to gain nuance and subtlety

- Read to develop arguments

- Read to find stimulating conversation partners and 'surprising friends'

- Read to find out what the opposition says

10. Using the Bible in theology essays

Perhaps I have placed the caboose before the train here. While you are plunging into Barth and Bray and Augustine, have you forgotten to read the most vital and authoritative text of all for doing theology – especially as Protestants think about it?

Well, yes. I hoped you had already begun your investigation into what Scripture has to say on your topic in your brainstorming phase. And as you read the theologians, I hope you were keeping in mind that the bar against which you are to be measuring them as successful theologians is the word of God. What's more, their usefulness to you, remember, is not least in the way the great theologians of church history alert you to how to read the Bible well.

But your theology essay is essentially an exercise in reading Scripture as a whole. It's a response to God's revelation of himself in the gospel of Jesus Christ – and we learn about that exclusively in the pages of Scripture. It's 'exegetical reason', to recall John Webster's phrase.

Notice what this isn't. It isn't the imposition of a system of thought on top of Scripture. It isn't trying to squeeze square pegs into round holes. I know a lot of professional biblical scholars who suspect that that's exactly what theology is on about.

And it can be, sometimes. But it shouldn't be: good theology drawn from Scripture is systematic in the sense that it tries to see the connection between the various teachings of Scripture. That's your task.

And your task is to look at the whole of the canon of Scripture. Pitting one Scripture against another, and then selecting your favourite option is not ultimately a Christian way to read Scripture. Of course, a lot of contemporary biblical scholarship has read the Bible as if it were a cacophony of disagreeing voices. This is not the place to discuss this sort of claim. But while the Scripture is a diverse book, it is also a unified one. And that unity is disclosed in Christ.

This is a way of saying that you should have in your armoury a view of the Scripture as a whole and how you should interpret the parts of Scripture in the light of the whole if you are going to do theology biblically. And the place of Christ in it is going to be central.

And that conviction about what Holy Scripture is drives the way you use it. The habit you need to avoid is the habit of collecting a series of isolated texts that then form great lists supposedly confirming your theological statements. But that's not a way to use Scripture that conforms to what Scripture actually is. You need to stand back and take a wide view of the grand sweep of the narrative of Scripture and ask: 'What is this grand story of God's interaction with the world telling me about the question?' There will be texts that demand inclusion in your thinking of course – but these need to be read theologically: that is, with an awareness of their place in the narrative of the Bible. You can't read the prophetic writings, for example, without reading them in the light of the Christ they foreshadowed.

I thought I'd pull out a paragraph from one of my undergraduate essays to illustrate what you are looking for in terms of Scripture:

> In the resurrection humanity receives both redemption and transformation. The broad scope of the resurrection is indicated by the analogy in the New Testament between God's creation ex nihilo and his salvific action (John 1, Rom 4:17). It is not surprising that the two concepts should be so associated, for the resurrection is a demonstration of God's absolute sovereignty over creation (as proclaimed in the Old Testament) and his appointment of Jesus as its ruler. The testimony of the apostles in Acts is to the Lordship of the resurrected Christ (2:32-36; 17:30-31 et al). The resurrection is, of course, key to Paul's cosmic eschatology (cf 1 Cor 15:20-8). To confess the resurrection is parallel to a confession of Jesus' Lordship (Rom 10:9).

Now, I have used Scripture in this paragraph in several ways – but I think consistently. My second sentence makes a rather sweeping claim, but grounds it on two texts – one a reference to a whole chapter, the other to a specific verse. In the third sentence I make statements about the resurrection and about what the Old Testament as a whole teaches. I do not cite a specific text, but I use Scripture certainly to ground my thinking on. The third, fourth and fifth sentences use texts which they quickly explain – so I say what Acts 2:32-36 and 17:30-31 say rather than merely cite them.

Now, to say that your theology essay ought to be properly and thoroughly scriptural does not allow you to indulge in the vice of prooftexting. What is prooftexting, and why don't I like it? Didn't I do a bit of it in the passage from my essay above?

Well ok, yes I did, a bit. Prooftexting is when you pull out a statement and then offer a list of Bible verses to back it up, in brackets. Some essayists actually seem to believe that offering this list actually is what making your essay scriptural means. (There are some terrible examples of published works that do it).

Why don't I like it?

1. Instead of drawing my attention to the text of Scripture, it actually makes me skip over it and move on. It makes me think I know what the Bible says when I don't.

2. SO OFTEN, when I look up the verses in a list, they don't say what the author claims they self-evidently say. Or, they say it in a very, very different way. Or, a subtle point is lost. It makes no allowance for genre, for context, for the difficult work of exegesis and so on.

3. It looks messy. (OK, that's not so important!)

4. It treats the Bible like a bank of data to be mined, and not a narrative of salvation-history. I would like there to be a ban on the phrase 'biblical data'. The Bible is NOT data!

5. It means a tendency to prefer 'direct-statement' evidence in theological argument over the testimony of say, the character of God revealed in his mighty acts, or the nature of the literary and biblical-theological context.

A great example of this is Isaiah 45:7.

> *I form the light and create darkness,*
> *I bring prosperity and create disaster;*
> *I, the LORD, do all these things.*

– which apparently looks like it charges God with direct agency in evil. I've seen it cited in lists of Bible references as a proof text to this end. But this short-cuts an enormously complex and very serious exegetical AND theological discussion which needs to be had. What's the biblical-theological context here? To whom is this prophecy addressed? Should we allow for hyperbole here?

What I do instead is that I try to quote the actual words of a particular text, and refer to those. This is not without its own difficulties, but I think it is preferable. I have even seen texts from Job's comforters cited in lists of prooftexts – when their views are precisely those being satirised by the book of Job!!

The bottom line is this: you need to show where necessary that you are aware of differences in interpretation – and if necessary, argue for yours.

Things tend to go horribly wrong most often when there is a controversial issue on the table that the student feels they have to defend polemically and aggressively. But your academic essay is not the place for such polemics. You need to show that you have considered the evidence – including the biblical evidence – carefully and maturely. Why have others comes to a different view on the interpretation of the biblical witness?

As a marker, I tend to smell a rat when a student keeps insisting that 'the Bible clearly says' and then simply asserting that it is so on a particular issue without any argument. That isn't to say that their interpretation isn't in fact the best one: but it requires establishing with careful scholarship. For example: there is a lot of heat in the issue of 'hell' (sorry!). But it simply is not the case that the 'conscious eternal torment' position is self-evidently the right one. Annihilationists have made a case for their side from Scripture. And if you want to argue for c.e.t. you have to counter their claims. You can't just shout louder than them, or suggest that they are all soft and deniers of the gospel. That might be true (or not), but they have made a case from the texts that requires serious consideration and careful response (whether to agree or disagree with them).

And that means getting all your bib studs skills out and wielding them. Greek and Hebrew – the works. Look up commentaries. Take into account the genre, the context, and so on. Then bring the text to the table and offer it as evidence for your theological case.

Neither should you indulge in word studies. A word study is a method whereby you take a word that appears in the Bible, and you analyse how it is used there. A valid exercise up to a point of course –

43

although it is worth pointing out that the Bible is an ancient book that uses everyday words, and non-biblical evidence is necessary to grasp the full range of meanings possible.

But a word study is not theology. Theology deals with concepts. Words of course are component parts of concepts. But just analysing the biblical words for love, or the instances that your Bible software tells you that agape is used, will not give you a biblical theology of love. Quite apart from that, it is bad linguistics, because context is always the trump card over the dictionary when it comes to the meaning of words. Next time you hear a skateboarder call something 'sick' or 'wicked' you'll get what I mean.

Righto – I've had a rant about proof texting and word studies (argh!) and I have made the point about reading the Bible as a whole, but I still need to say more. I still encounter a great degree of skepticism about the discipline of theology amongst evangelical Christians, even very well educated and thoughtful ones. And this is because they feel that theology asks questions about which the text of Scripture isn't directly concerned or says things without making apparently direct reference to the text of Scripture.

I appreciate the concern. Whereas the besetting sin of biblical studies is to get lost in the labyrinths of unanswerable and irrelevant historical questions, so the great vice of theology or doctrine is to follow the trail of bread crumbs leading up philosophical passageways to no clear or important destination.

Theology is, as Webster explained (and see above), 'exegetical reason'. Its job is simply faithfulness to Scripture. But in working out faithfulness to Scripture it will seek to probe the concepts that Scripture introduces, and to articulate them with precision and depth and clarity. It works with Scripture as a whole.

This I've said already. But we have to realise just how difficult this is. This is not simply a matter on each question of finding the simple proof texts and citing them. It is thinking through 'what is consistent with the God of Scripture and his mighty acts in the world'?

That's why we refer to this thing called 'orthodoxy' – because it gives us a set of intuitions, already carefully worked out, with which to begin our theological work on Scripture. We don't read Scripture alone, but in the company of a great number of faithful Bible readers before us. And the consensus of the Christian church down the ages is that God is triune – three persons in one God. That is not, per se, the explicit testimony of Scripture. It is an inference drawn from Scripture and summarised in the great creeds of the Church. When you read Scripture and attempt a piece of Christian theology, you can legitimately begin with this as your presupposition and work from there.

Discovering the relations between the three persons, and between the acts of God in history and his transcendent being is a valid theological task which may involve passages of thought without proof texts. Yet it can be thoroughly, profoundly scriptural – because it is taking the essential testimony of Scripture as a whole and working out how it is coherent and how it applies in our world.

For example: British theologian Colin Gunton makes the interesting observation that the unity and the diversity of the triune God who is at the heart of reality is neither a form of monism (all is one) nor a way of seeing the world as sheer unconnected chaos. The trinity – a doctrine established by a reading of the whole of Scripture and not from merely a set of proof texts or from a single text – provides a challenge in this way to both a tyrannical modernism and its postmodern opposite.

Another example is this: the 'openness of God' movement was a group of evangelical theologians who taught that God is 'open' to the future – that he changes, grows and indeed learns, and that he carries out his plans in reaction to what occurs in history as much as according to his foreordination. As evangelicals, this group of theologians claimed that the Bible was on their side – and so it certainly seems to be on a surface reading of some passages of the Old Testament. Doesn't God 'change his mind' or 'repent' in Exodus 32:14, for example?

And yet what they taught was a deviation from classic Christian orthodoxy. So what? Well, I am happy to grant that orthodoxy is open to revision if you can provide enough force from Scripture to establish that it needs to be. But orthodoxy – those theological convictions worked out in the first few centuries of the Christian church – also gives you a way of reading Scripture such that we ought to read much of the Bible's language of God changing and so on in an analogical way. It isn't a straightforward case of God changing his mind. We cannot, according to orthodoxy, always move directly from scriptural statements about God to direct claims about his nature without first interpreting them in the light of what the orthodox doctrine of God says about him.

This means that you have more work to do than you may have thought to get your theology essay cooking on the stove. All the worst heretics have been Bible readers who claimed that Scripture supported their case and could point to proof texts that supported them. To defeat them, you need to show how what they say doesn't fit with the whole of Scripture and isn't consistent with Christian orthodoxy (which itself derives from Scripture).

What this means by the way for your reading of theologians is this: they may not cite a whole lot of texts directly, but they still might be Bible theologians. You can still be faithful to Scripture by working out the concepts of Christian orthodoxy. This is simply a way of reading Scripture – and is subject of course to the text of Scripture as its authority. But simply saying 'hey, there's not a whole lot of Bible references here' doesn't tell me anything about the scriptural faithfulness or otherwise of a writer.

Like I said: all the worst heretics have been Bible guys.

In sum:

- You have to read Scripture as a whole to do theology biblically
- Orthodoxy helps you to read Scripture theologically
- Avoid prooftexting and word studies

II. How to treat your opponents

OK everyone: gather in. Shut down Facebook, switch off your phone. I'm getting serious now. This is a biggie, I think.

Here it is:

You need to treat your opponents with charity and respect.

Yep – that's right: in your essay you need to give your opponents a fair hearing – as fair a hearing as you possibly can.

I know it's likely that you've signed up for theological study because you think there is a right and a wrong, and because you are passionately committed with all your being to the truth of the gospel and the authority of the Bible. I know you've probably been inspired by preachers in your life who painted things in black and white terms, and who pointed to the false teachers out there and told you to beware.

BUT: it is a) a matter of basic ethics and b) a matter of academic good practice to treat those with whom you disagree as fairly as possible.

Ethics? That's right. You need to treat people as you would want to be treated. You are not a tabloid journalist. You would hate it if:

a) your views were heard at second hand and no-one ever asked you what you thought in person in your own words

b) it was assumed that you were trying to deceive people and acting in bad faith

c) it was assumed that you were trying to avoid the clear statements of the Bible

d) a caricature of your views were offered, then dismissed in a glib sentence

But – can I say this? – that is how many theology students treat their opponents in their essays. It is actually a matter not only for changing techniques, but for repentance in my view. It is that serious.

Now hear me right: I am not saying 'go soft on naughty liberals' or something. It is in fact the opposite: if ideas are influential and credible then to respond to them properly so that the people of God are well served we ought to take great care to treat them ethically. It is the seriousness of the matter that in fact demands that we don't resort to cheap shots, polemics and over-heated rhetoric.

Don't put these in your essay.

And it is actually bad academic practice. It makes your argument look weak if you do this. I once read a sheaf of essays on Karl Barth most of which did not show any attempt to engage with him at first hand. Most of them used an essay by Roger Nicole to summarise Barth's arguments, and then, surprise surprise, dismissed Barth in the terms Nicole did. Now, Nicole was a fine scholar: but Barth is a major thinker whose writing you need to deal with AT FIRST HAND or not at all. Sure, you can read Nicole. But not to read Barth in this case? Fail. Seriously. The big 'F'. Makes me cross, that does.

If you put up a caricature of your opponent, and then argue the caricature down, what have you demonstrated? Precisely nothing. In addition, you need to ask: is there nothing that can be learnt from this person? Barth himself was a great critic of the 19th century theologian Friedrich Schleiermacher. But he once said something along the lines of 'you cannot hate here until you have loved'. It was precisely because Barth knew Schleiermacher at first hand and could appreciate what he was trying to do that made him such a devastating critic of Schleiermacher's work. That's a model worth aspiring to.

This flaw of lack of charity also reveals an often unwarranted overconfidence in your own position. The person who is dismissive of the other person 'because the Bible clearly teaches otherwise' usually hasn't done the hard work to establish that the Bible does in fact teach what they think it does. Have they actually heard the case for the other side? Often not, I am afraid.

In sum:

- Treat your opponents with respect
- Avoid cheap shots and caricature

12.   Some advice on quoting

You probably know that quoting is part of the essay writing shebang. An essay's gotta have quotes, right, to show that you've read things – hasn't it?

But quotations can get way out of hand. They can be over-complicated, over-long and poorly chosen. Or, there can be just too many of them – so you can't see the argument for the quotes. As my supervisor once said,

I don't like there to be too many quotes.

Wise words.

There are three reasons that you should permit yourself the indulgence of a quotation.

1) *The other author completely nailed it.* That is, they have put something SO beautifully that you couldn't possibly put it that way yourself. You just have to put it in. Example "As Karl Barth put it: 'This man is man.'" Notice that it is short, and pithy. No pith, no quote.

Don't put in a quote that is full of jargon that you don't understand. That use does NOT fulfil this rule! As a general rule, write something around the quote that shows you DO understand it.

2) *Yes, my opponent actually does say that.* If your opponent has an outrageous point of view and you are trying to engage it, use quotation to illustrate and exemplify – just so we can see that you aren't misrepresenting her or him.

3) *I am expounding this point of view to learn from it.* If you are trying to explain what Luther's view on justification was, so that you can learn from it, throw in a couple of short quotes to pick up his voice, his language.

The golden rule is – KEEP IT SHORT. Quotes that take up 10 or more lines are just padding. Summarise the idea and put in a footnote.

And, as I said above: introduce and follow the quote with enough explanatory words to show that you know what it means.

What work is the quote doing for you? What was I supposed to get from it as a reader? Just because a well-known author said it doesn't mean it is a) right b) intelligible c) what you want to say.

Also: watch that your quote doesn't introduce new material into your essay that is just confusing. Clip the quote so it is PRECISELY relevant to your case and so that there is no extra material.

BUT: do read carefully. Sometimes an author is recounting someone else's argument. If you pull out a quote from the middle of such a passage, you will badly distort the views of the author. Take care!

In sum:

- Use quotations sparingly
- Quote if:
    - o   The author nailed it
    - o   You want to prove your opponent really does say that
    - o   You are expounding a view to learn from it
- Quote SHORT
- Quote faithfully to the author

13. Types of argument for your essay

Talking about quotations is getting ahead of ourselves though.

Let's say that you've begun researching the topic area, you've made some extensive notes and now you are feeling that the time has come to write. What are you going to write?

Remember at this stage what I said in the beginning: an essay is an argument about something trying to show your skills in the analysis of texts and the synthesis of ideas. That is to say: you need to argue something. Before you start writing, ask yourself this absolutely crucial question: what am I arguing for? What thesis am I proposing and defending?

It will help you no end if you sit down, right now, and thrash out a single sentence – a sentence that is clear to you, and that takes a position. Be a little bit brave, even. Go on – what's life for, if not to live a little dangerously?

Actually, I am quite serious: a little courage in framing your argument is a good thing. You can always modify your statement as you go along. What you are putting up is a working thesis – that is, it is something for your essay to lean against while you write it. You may at the end of the process come back and change your thesis entirely.

Now, consider these two images:

On the right you have the classic on/off switch. It only has two positions: on and, well, off. You can switch it on. And you can switch it off. That's really all it does.

On the left is another design classic: the volume knob. It has 10 numbers which indicate a spectrum of positions. (It may even have 11, but that's another story, one about Marshall stacks, and so on.)

Now: you might be a personality that prefers everything in the world to be a matter of on or off. Yes or no. Black and white (you knew I was going to say that, right?).

But the thing is that in an argument in which you are trying to convince the marker of your ability to make subtle distinctions, you really have to operate as if the world had volume knobs on it rather than on/off switches. That is: there may be degrees of certainty, elements of moderation, and many other ways of sitting between the extremes on a spectrum that give your essay greater persuasive power. This is partly because sitting at one extreme is often claiming far more than you can possibly establish in your short piece.

Let me take you back to one of our sample questions:

Is 'conscious eternal torment' the only sound biblical and theological description of the nature of hell?

You can see that this question is actually inviting you to take an extreme position – the word 'only' is the giveaway. But it would be a bit of a trap to accept that invitation. It would show a degree of analytical sophistication if you were rather to argue that (if this is your opinion) 'conscious eternal torment' is the most convincing interpretation of the biblical material. Instead of using your on/off switch, you've used your volume dial – and you've settled on a 9 on that dial perhaps, but you've used a much more nuanced way of measuring the results of your study.

How are you going to argue for your thesis? Arguments can take various shapes. Here are some:

1) **The cumulative argument** is an argument that is in effect constituted by a list of points that do not necessarily relate to one another but that, when added all together, make the case. Because you don't have to say how the points relate, the cumulative argument is a very simple form to use – it works well in exams especially. Its weakness is that it doesn't make for a logical whole;

and if you don't treat each piece of evidence carefully, it can look like each piece has equal weight – which is unlikely. The other problem is how you might deal with objections and counterarguments – but you can do this under each point as you go through.

2) **The sparring partner argument** is an argument in which you chiefly wrestle with the argument of another in a critical way. What you need to do here is offer an in depth AND FAIR exposition of their work and then engage with it, modifying it as you see fit. Don't worry about originality – even a small adjustment can be a new perspective on the problem. Your wrestle with the sparring partner may lead to fresh insights. It could be that the thinker is from a very different perspective than your own – and adapting their work critically leads to a very provocative synthesis. The danger of course is that you become intimidated or overwhelmed by the sparring partner.

3) **The thesis proposed and dissected argument** is one that I have found theologian John Webster using. He starts with a detailed proposition and then takes it apart element by element, before putting it back together at the end. This argument can be aesthetically quite tidy and also means that you concentrate on concepts that hang together rather than bits from here and there.

4) **The evaluate the alternatives on the table** argument immediately plunges you into the tradition of the discussion of the matter at hand and shows your awareness of the secondary literature discussion. You can explain each alternative, offer an evaluation according to strengths and weaknesses, and then offer your own synthesis, or choose the strongest option. The danger is that if you don't do a good job of describing the alternatives the whole thing looks like a mess.

TIP: you know those 'Three/Four/Five Views On' books? Do take great care when using these: they are designed for people just like you and they are inviting you to take a huge shortcut. Some students think they can do their entire research from one of these books. The essays are inevitably of uneven quality in these books. And what's more: I think they leave students feeling completely confused. I know *I* feel confused.

In sum:

* Volume knobs, not on/off switches

14. The classic introduction

Have you ever been speed dating? No, I didn't think so. Me neither. But the point of speed dating is to get a quick but true glimpse of someone: an introduction to them. Introductions open little windows on the souls of others so we can catch a glimpse of what might be inside. They are a beginning, perhaps.

Or maybe, they are enough: we all hope that we are good enough to make a rapid judgment about someone so that we can screen out any psychopaths that might really not be good people to get to know; but the trouble with this is that psychopaths, it turns out, are by definition extraordinarily good at the kind of superficial charm that you don't notice is superficial until you scratch below the surface and discover something really alarming, like a collection of stuffed animals, or the entire Barry Manilow back catalogue.

By then it is usually much too late.

So it is with your essay. Not the psychopath bit. Your introduction is meant to serve as a window into the rest of the piece. And it has three important functions:

1) Your introduction should set the scene and frame the question. Briefly show that you have understood the question and why it is a question worth asking. Who is asking it? Why should we care? What is at stake? There needs to be a bit of drama here – a sense of conflict even. In a couple of crisp sentences tell us where the question has come from and why the reader has to read on. Be a bit alluring. *Flirt* with me! (Ahem. Just in case you are taking this a bit too literally, there are strict rules about that sort of thing!)

2) Your introduction should state your answer to the question. I'm sorry, but unless you are some kind of essay writing genius, this is a rule I pretty much insist upon. Most of us don't have the skill to create the kind of essay that only reveals its answer to the question at the end. This isn't a whodunnit. If you tell me upfront what the endpoint is, I'll have a way of making sense of what comes next in the essay. I'll have a point on which to hang all your loose ends, and it won't look like your essay is meandering. It gives it focus.

3) Your introduction should give an indication of how you are going to answer the question. Yep, tell me your method. What's the procedure that's going to follow? And what structure are you going to use? Again, you can do this in summary form of course. But be explicit about what you are doing: first this, then this, and lastly this. This helps the reader pace themselves.

I cannot tell you what a difference this makes to the essay. If you have a good introduction you'll write a good essay, pretty much. It is that simple. So why do 70% of students not do it? They write no introduction. Or they only do one of the above. Then they wonder why no one asks them on a date...

In sum:

- Your introduction should set the scene and frame the question

- Your introduction should state your answer to the question

- Your introduction should give an indication of how you are going to answer the question

15. Why presentation matters, and how to make it work for you

Now I am a person who likes to think I can see past a person's halitosis, bulbous proboscis and liver spots to their true character. I don't like to think I am swayed by outward appearances.

Truth is, I am.

This is true as a marker, as well. I do not usually take marks off for shoddy presentation (though many institutions do). But I am sure that shoddy presentation affects how I perceive the essay, and how I perceive the efforts of the author, even if subconsciously. So – make presentation work for you, not against you.

Partly, this is just a courtesy of communication. You have been asked to communicate in a certain way, and it is just polite to do so. Most theological colleges and seminaries will have pretty strict guidelines about how you present your essay – how you format your footnotes, and so on. Find out what they are – and (I don't know, here's a novel idea) follow them. If you can't follow them: then at least be self-consistent – that creates a better impression than a random formatting performance!

So then: a few tips on formatting and presentation:

1) **Don't save paper.** With electronic submission of assignments it is ridiculous to see tiny fonts and tiny margins on an assignment. It costs nobody anything to make it look much more readable! Even if you are submitting your work on paper, a couple of extra pages isn't going to destroy the Amazon. Most colleges like double spacing and, if printed out, single sided.

2) **Author-date or ...?** Often you are allowed a choice of formatting for references. People from a science background prefer the author-date system, with the reference placed in the text in brackets instead of using a footnote (though it can be used in a footnote as well). This is becoming popular in biblical Studies as well. My preference, personally, as an Arts graduate, is for the humanities style of referencing, in which you give a footnote and then a full reference the first time you use a text (abbreviated on subsequent uses).

56

I am not going to go into the details of explaining them here, because each institution will have its own way of requiring you to do this. If you have the freedom to use the author-date, and it works for you – feel free. Whatever you do, don't use endnotes – the references should be on the page where they are made. Otherwise it is just a source of marker grumpiness.

3) **Reference styles.** An earnest plea: do take care to follow the guidelines in citing books and articles and other works. Usually, if you mention a book, you italicise the title. If it's an article, you put it in inverted commas. Simple. I would say that a quarter of students don't do this – why? Baffling.

4) **Font.** Now, this is a bit controversial. Use a serif font – because it looks smarter. By which I mean – more intelligent. I am dead serious here. You might be a fan of Arial or Calibri. That's great for you. But if you want to look like a scholar, use a font with the little curly bits. Even boring ole Times New Roman is fine. Or Garamond, Bookman, Perpetua, Constantia. Don't make it a silly font, of course, and only use one font in your whole piece. But make it a serif font. Academic studies have been carried out on this which show that the perception of your piece as a piece of scholarship is affected by the font you choose! Of course, as a marker I pay no conscious attention to the font you choose ... But if there's a choice between one impression and another – why not give yourself every chance?

5) **Paragraphs.** I usually like to right and left justify my writing so that you get a nice square block of text. To me, left-only justifying looks untidy. But do allow for a space in between paragraphs. Not a huge gap, such that they look disconnected. But make for a gap nonetheless. I personally don't think an indent in a paragraph of type looks tidy, and if you already have a space between your paragraphs, it is unnecessary.

Oh, and do make your paragraphs of roughly even length – they should be between 2 and 5 sentences long, or about 200 words. If one paragraph is a monster, consider chopping it in half. There's almost always a way to do this. A paragraph should be a coherent unit of thought. If you have a new thought, start a new paragraph.

6) **Attend to punctuation and spelling.** For some people, it seems, punctuation and spelling don't matter a great deal. Again, they are

not essential to the content of your essay. But in the days of spell checkers and so on, there really is no excuse for persistently bad spelling. I'll have some things to say about punctuation in a later section. But just to give you a taste: remember, there's a huge difference between 'Let's eat, Grandma' and 'Let's eat Grandma'....

7) **Print it nicely.** If you are printing it out, can you find a printer which doesn't produce a faded line down the middle of the page?

8) **Use a clear and consistent system of headings.** You don't have to use headings at all, of course. But if you do, make them neat and tidy. Don't make them excessively large, or colourful. If your text is 12 point, make them at most 14 point. Otherwise they shout at the reader.

Presentation is all about not distracting your reader. Why wouldn't you go and preach in a gold lamé t-shirt and g-string combo? Because I think it would be rather diverting... Presentation is about focusing attention on the content of your essay and, strangely, not on your presentation. None of these rules of presentation make your essay a successful essay. But it is interesting that it is almost always the case that the best essays are also nicely presented. I think it reveals something about your state of mind as your approach the essay.

In sum:

- Presentation does matter
- The essential principle: don't distract your reader

16.   How to write well in a theology essay

The medium of expression for your essay is the written word, in the form of the traditional 'essay' or 'research paper' or whatever your institution labels it.

I assume, pretty much, that if you are going into Christian ministry and you have chosen to study theology, then you don't mind a few words here and there. In fact, I reckon it is part of your vocation to be a student of words. You will be exercising teaching gifts using words. So knowing how to communicate in written language is a skill worth honing.

It is all about judging what register to use in the right situation. What do I mean? Register is basically how you pitch your language according to the context. Is it highly formal? Is it chatty? Is it conversational? That will be a factor of the register.

The essay is an exercise in formal writing in an academic setting. That is, you are seeking as much precision as you can muster and assuming that your audience is a very well educated person in the field in which you are writing. You can use technical language, complex sentences, and elevated vocabulary – in fact, you ought to. You can assume that your reader will work hard to try to understand you.

You are aiming to be persuasive – but you are not in the pulpit. Many theological students find it hard to step out of the pulpit, I've noticed! Persuasion in this instance doesn't mean the kind of hyped-up rhetorical language you might use in a sermon. In fact, the opposite is true here: you need to keep the emotive impact of your words in check. Persuasion is by dint of reasoning here. Leave the hyperbole for Sunday.

Even though you are writing academic prose, this does not absolve you of the responsibility to be as clear as you possibly can. Clarity doesn't mean simplicity, or dumbing-it-down. It doesn't mean writing in a conversational way. It does mean making your sentences hang together well, making your paragraphs clearly about something and giving us an obvious sense of where you are going in the essay. You aren't out to win a Pulitzer prize, here. It doesn't need to be fancy prose. But it is amazing how a bit of attention to the writing really helps the essay – because to write well is to think well.

So, my first piece of advice will be: re-read your work, aloud if you can. And ask yourself: is it clear to me what I mean? If you can't follow what you are saying, don't expect that I will. You need to use your ears: does it sound right? That's always a good first test of your writing.

These are a few of the things you can do to make your writing more clear:

1) **See if you can cut your sentences in half**. Sometimes sentences just try to do too much, and the structure of the sentence can't bear the weight of meaning your are forcing on it. The full stop (period) is your friend.

2) **Take care how you use the 'connector' words**: but, yet, however, therefore, nevertheless. These words are important cues to the reader. But they can also be completely confusing, especially if they are used in a haphazard fashion.

   NB 'however' is not a conjunction. You don't use it in the middle of a sentence to co-ordinate two thoughts. It is an adverb, and usually goes first or second in a sentence and is followed by a comma. So: not 'I went to the shops to buy a pie, however I discovered that they were closed', but 'I went to the shops to buy a pie. However, I discovered that they were closed'.

3) **Start each paragraph** with a sentence indicating what the paragraph is about. End each paragraph by saying what you have just concluded from the paragraph.

4) **Prefer active to passive**. This hint is a standard of textbooks on writing everywhere. It isn't a 100% rule. But you save words by using the active. For that reason I say to you that yes, you CAN use 'I' in an essay. The reason professors don't like I is that we are not much interested in your feelings: 'I feel that xyz'; nor in your opinions: 'I think that xyz'. We don't want to know what you feel. We want to know the truth!

   The problem is that not using 'I' results in all kinds of contortions that just sound wrong: 'In this essay it will be shown that'.... Yuck. Errgh. I think it is perfectly acceptable to say what you are doing: 'I will show that...'.

And it is clear.

An essay is an attempt to find some clarity of thought on a subject. The following list of words are obstacles in the way of clarity of thought. When you find yourself using them, catch yourself and ask 'what am I really trying to say here?' – and then say that instead, without the bad word.

1. *important* (in what way? to whom?)

2. *helpful* (who is being 'helped'? helpful to do what exactly? 'Helpful' is a word that preachers should stop using, too)

3. *significant* (to whom? so what?)

4. *useful* (how? who cares? useful for what purpose?)

5. *interesting* (how so? I am not interested at the moment just because you say this is interesting…)

Remember, these are tips rather than rules: but I notice how often these words become a shorthand for 'I don't quite know what to say here'. In particular, an essay calls you to make judgements – which many of us are afraid to do. What does 'useful' commit you to? Nothing at all! Scrub it and find something better to say.

Don't be afraid of metaphors either, or of using visual language to describe what you are doing in your argument. It is amazing to reflect on how prominent metaphors have been in advancing discoveries in the world of science – the notion of a 'field', for example (as in 'gravitational field'). This is because metaphors have the power to yolk ideas together in new ways and thus show us something we haven't seen before. Don't be over the top with it, of course; and don't used tired metaphors that have become stock-in-trade. But a fresh image will open up all kinds of possibilities of thought.

Now I am afraid that I have to have a word with you about punctuation. I'm really not a punctuation fascist. Well, I used not to be, until I had to mark lots of theology essays. And I discovered: it just is simply the case that bad punctuation is a threat to civilisation itself. We punctuate our sentences for the same reason that we use cutlery and wear pants. Take the comma, for example: mostly, people just fill up a pepperpot with commas and then grind them over the page, so that they fall at random. Writing ought to have commas, they think. So, commas it shall have!

Now there are different schools of comma usage. I am a comma minimalist. Mostly, I think you can do without most of the ones we commonly use. I am not going to go through the uses of the comma here because you can easily find help on the web. (My favourite is http://grammar.quickanddirtytips.com/.) Do yourself the favour of checking those out before you go comma sprinkling.

Likewise, do check out the rules for using apostrophes (notice, not 'apostrophe's'). This one is dead easy and should take you a minute to learn. It becomes confusing to read work in which plurals and possessives are all mixed up. And it looks kind of highschoolish!

The best advice with punctuation is to use your ears – but not always. And when in doubt, see if a full stop will help things. You can be *too* aural – many people punctuate their essays as if they were spoken pieces rather than written. This is particularly grievous when they put a comma in instead of a full stop.

The last thing I would say about becoming a better writer is this: *be a reader of great writing.* In the end, I can give you tips to improve the clarity of your writing, but the best way to become a good writer is to expose yourself to good writing. Often, I have to say, theologians are terrible writers – or, we read their work in translation from German or Latin. You aren't going to learn to write from them. You are, however, going to improve your ability to write by picking up a George Eliot novel, or a Jane Austen, or an Ernest Hemingway. (Find the English or History major in your class and ask them what they are reading!)

And anyhow, as a developing theologian, you should be cultivating the reading life. A young pastor I know has committed himself to reading for an hour a day – theology mostly, but certainly not only. While his example is outstanding, I am alarmed when I ask theological students in interviews whether they consider themselves a reader or not to find that most say 'not really'. I am alarmed because these are people who are going to have words as the tools of their trade – shouldn't they take every opportunity to sharpen them?

So what I am asking here is for a lifestyle choice. Become a reader – not because it means you will sail through your theology essays, but because you will be a much better servant of the Lord Jesus Christ if you are.

In sum:

- Be a reader of great writing
- Don't be afraid of metaphors
- Learn the simple rules of English punctuation
- Be clear, and avoid vague words

17.   The art of signposting

The greatest essays come off because they are an integrated whole. They keep the reader's attention the whole way through – not because they have sparkling prose (though that's nice) but because they connect the ideas together well.

That is: they keep reminding the reader where they are in the argument, so the chances of getting lost are minimized. This is of course a very helpful discipline for writers, because it asks them to ask themselves – 'where am I up to? What does this bit contribute to the whole of the essay?'

There are a few ways to do this.

1) **Use headings**. I used to be opposed to headings in essays, chiefly because I was a snob about such things. ('Surprise me', I hear you say). But I have changed. The use of a few headings can, with a minimum of words, communicate to the reader the structure of your piece quite brilliantly and elegantly. Now, I don't mean that every paragraph should have a heading. I would also counsel against points and subpoints and futher subpoints. That's just confusing. But if there are five identifiable phases of your essay, why not signpost them with a system of headings? It's economical and it keeps everyone up to speed.

2) **Use summative sentences**. You may have just stepped your way through a very complex argument involving exegesis, historical theology and a jab at Eberhard Jüngel for good measure. But when you come to a section break, don't assume that I have followed this all the way through – or that I can see what it contributes to the whole. *Tell me.*

They say when you begin to act that you should overact – that the stage requires you to magnify your actions so that the audience knows clearly what you are doing. Likewise, in an essay, you need to overact a bit: telling me explicitly what each bit of your essay has just done in a brief summative statement. And it is kind to exhausted markers.

3) **Use questions that flow**. A great way to ensure continuity is to introduce the next section of your piece with a question that comes

out of the previous bit – which may also have been introduced by a question. Paul does this in his letters to brilliant effect – 'What shall we say then: shall we go on sinning, that grace may increase?' (Romans 6:1 NIV) And you can follow his argument by stages because he signposts it with questions which he then proceeds to answer.

In sum:

- Use headings

- Use summative sentences

- Use questions that flow

18. Bringing home the bacon

The jet plane of your essay has left the tarmac and cruised at altitude for several thousand words. Now it is time to land this baby. I don't know if you've been on a plane when the passengers break out into spontaneous applause the moment the plane is safely on the runway. That always rather bothered me – are there landings that don't earn such applause? Could the pilot be persuaded by a lack of applause not to try so hard the next time he flies? I'd rather landing be a kind of take-it-for-granted expectation, wouldn't you?

In any case, you as the pilot of your essay have a job to do to make sure everything ends well. A good strong conclusion can leave a lasting impression that you were in control of your material, that no threads were left untied, and that you had a clear mind as to the argument you were pursuing.

Most often a conclusion will be a paragraph that adds nothing new to the essay but just makes for a clean finish. This is the most basic form of conclusion. Don't introduce a new writer to quote, or a new piece of information, or a new angle on the question. Return to the question itself, and make sure you have the terms of the question included in the way you phrase your conclusion – don't leave anyone in anyone doubt that you have actually answered the question.

But there's another way to go here, especially if you have a bit of space. Why not consider for a while what the implications or possible implications of your argument are? Having established your argument, now consider: what does this mean in terms of your theological thinking more generally? Theology is a discipline that hangs together. Each bit affects every other bit. If you establish something in eschatology, for example, it will have implications for your doctrine of creation. You will always have something to say at this point. If you have decided that the resurrection of Jesus *was* indeed bodily, and established this from a convincing theological argument, then ask: *what will this mean for our doctrine of creation? What will this mean for how we think about salvation?*

Often, this is the chance to bring some ethical observations to bear by asking: what does this mean for the life of church or the life of the individual believer in the world? What difference does this argument make in those contexts?

This is a chance to be bold and imaginative. You can insure yourself against the risk of being a bit speculative here by giving a slight moderation or qualification to your statements. It is perfectly acceptable to use the subjunctive here – 'it could be said', 'it might be the case', 'possibly', and so on. But you are showing yourself to have initiative and a bit of originality, so the risk is certainly worth it.

Do make sure with your conclusion that any promises you have made in your essay have been fulfilled. Go back over your essay and see if you can spot where you might have made a claim about what your essay will do – and then either make sure your essay has done this, or modify the claim according to what you actually have done! It might be that in your final paragraphs you have an opportunity to address those promises explicitly.

If you are short of words, your conclusion need not be long. A sentence might be enough. But an essay with no conclusion remains curiously unpersuasive. We are left asking 'what did it all amount to?' Make sure the reader knows exactly what it amounted to.

In sum:

- Your conclusion should add nothing new

- Make sure you have fulfilled any promises you have made

- If you do have some space, consider the implications of your essay for other areas of theology

19. What to do with it now

19.1. *Publishing your Essay – why not?*

An essay amounts to a great deal of work. Perhaps you spent 50 or more hours on it. It may have been a genuinely formative period for you as you worked through a theological issue at depth. You may have surprised yourself by finding that your mind has changed on a particular issue. Ministerial candidates often speak to me of their theology essay as a landmark in their formation as pastor-teachers. It seems a pity to let all that work only have a single reader – your marker.

What's more, it may be that the marking process has exposed some significant (or even just minor) flaws in your piece. It would be a pity to let the opportunity of revising the piece in the light of expert comment go to waste. Part of really learning is making the most of second chances.

You should ask yourself – what can I now do with this material?

That is not to say that every piece of theological essay work is ready for academic publication. By no means! But written publication takes many forms. And preparing for a public audience is a discipline that will refine your thinking even further.

So you need to take stock. It could be that your piece is truly outstanding and has been rewarded with the appropriate marks. This is still not to say that it is a piece of peer-reviewed material ready for the *Scottish Journal of Theology*, but perhaps it could be with a bit of spit and polish. Why not use some vacation time to really push the piece into the stratosphere? Take every bit of advice and criticism you can, and extend the work to give it a bit more depth perhaps. Ask your teachers what they would do. There are of course many journals that would publish work with not quite as much finesse – take *The Churchman*, or *Anvil*, *Trinity Journal* or *Reformed Theological Review*. These middle-weight journals might be a great place to put your work, and you'll find them usually receptive.

It could be, however, that your piece could be adapted to a magazine-style piece. This will need a bit of a change of tone, perhaps a sexier introduction, and a scalpel applied to some of your quotes and footnotes. Imagine an intelligent layperson as your reader, and try to explain the material to them. It will need a clear explanation of what the point of the exercise is. Make it into an article *The Briefing* or *Cross+Way* could publish – you could take their articles as a model perhaps.

You could of course self-publish, on a blog or somewhere else on line, perhaps. The advantage of blogging is that you get exposed to the withering criticism of anyone who happens to happen by. But you may have to publish your piece in parts in order to make it digestible.

Why not consider how the things you have learnt would go at a seminar or workshop at a conference? Again, the trick is to see if you can make the ideas you have come up with switch genres – and to see if you can sharpen up your ideas in the light of the feedback you have got from the marking process.

19.2. *Turning your piece in to a series of talks or sermons*

The other obvious way to make use of your hours of work is to turn your thoughts into a series of talks or sermons. Oh, I know: you just saw the eyes of the congregation glazing over.

But that needn't be. Naturally, you will need to package your ideas as a sermon and not merely as an essay. The great thing about having to do this is that you will need to distil what the key ideas you have written about are, and put them in language suitable for a church congregation to hear and understand.

There is far too little preaching on theological topics in my experience. There certainly is topical preaching. But it tends to be on practical issues rather than on, say, 'The Holy Spirit', or 'Creation'.

You may need to choose some key Scriptural texts and bounce off them rather than plunging into an abstract debate. I would be wary of introducing too much secondary material into a sermon, but by the same token congregations benefit greatly from knowing they are part of a two-millennia-long history of reflection on and contention for these issues.

What you will have to do is to consider how your topic impacts real life. What does it matter to the 'ordinary' person? Why does having their convictional world challenged and reshaped matter? Why should they be a party to it? Of course, this is as much a challenge to the preacher as it is to the congregation.

In sum:

- Don't be shy about thinking of ways in which your essay could have a second life

20.   A footnote about footnotes

(In everything that follows I should say at the outset that the first thing to do is to check the policy of your particular institution and follow that above all else.)

Someone once said to me that the perfect research essay would be one sentence long and the rest would be a single footnote.

I have no idea what they were drinking that night. I think they were having a go at the desperation some students have to slather everything in a thick butter of footnotes such that the actual text of the essay virtually disappears.

It is worth just clarifying what footnotes are there for. The chief purpose of them is to serve as a place to put your references. It is an efficient way of showing that your statements rest on the authority of someone else and that you have researched your essay well. Of course, the Author-Date system asks you to put your references in brackets in the text, so footnotes won't have that function then.

Do take care to make it clear how the reference relates to the text. If you've put a reference in at the end of the sentence, ask yourself: what is it doing there? Is it that the author I am citing agrees with this point? Or disagrees? Or – well, what? A couple of short words can do the job here. Put a 'so' in front of the reference, for example, and you have indicated that the author concurs, and the reader knows exactly what the reference I am using demonstrates.

One other use of footnotes is to provide a bit of protection. What do I mean? Indicate by means of a footnote where there are unexplored avenues. Let the reader know that you are aware of tracks you might have followed, but chose not to. Protect yourself from the flank attack – the attack which says 'weren't you aware of Augustine's views on the subject?'

Another purpose of footnotes is to provide interesting but non-essential commentary. Now you need to take great care here – don't put something actually creative and vital in your footnotes that should be in the text. I say to my research students whenever I see an extended footnote 'shouldn't this be in the text?' The footnote may be a sign of simple indecision on your part. If that's the case – decide!

A teacher of mine used to say 'footnotes should be fun'. I don't think he meant that this was the place to put a couple of jokes you have lately heard. Rather – if you have a genuinely interesting diversion, then this is the place for it.

But remember: don't try to hide, or look as if you are trying to hide, extra words in the footnotes. Most institutions will ask you to count footnotes in your final word count in any case.

In sum:

- Use footnote commentary sparingly

- Don't hide extra words in your footnotes

- Take care that the footnote relates clearly to the text

- Use footnotes to protect yourself by showing that you have read widely

Supplement: Writing theology exam essays

I am often requested to say something out about writing theology essays under exam conditions. The exam essay is a different beast with a different anatomy, though of the same species as the research essay. Here are some pointers:

1. **This is no place for perfectionists.** This is the frustration of the exam format for many people, but why I was quite good at them – me with my 'near-enough-is-good-enough' attitude. What you aren't going to write under exam conditions is theology for the ages. So have a cry and a (metaphorical) cup of tea, and get down to work. The point of the exam is usually to test a) the breadth of your knowledge and b) your ability to marshall theological evidence to answer a question.

2. **Prepare long term.** Weeks before your exam, refine your notes. Determine what will be on the exam – and do remember to cover yourself against the exam by preparing enough material to make sure you have an essay to write on each question. If you want to gamble, go put your pocket money on the horses. But as I say, refine your notes and other material so that for each topic area you have a single A4 sheet. On that sheet you should have: basic data; scriptural passages that are relevant; a couple of short quotes from great theologians or brief descriptions of their opinions. Make it neat! Use colours. Mind map if that floats your boat. Then: put everything else away. Just use the single A4 sheet from then on. Except:

3. **Two days before the exam.** Your short term memory is amazing, so make the most of it by doing a bit of cram-reading just before. Because you have your A4 sheet, you shouldn't have to stress here about memorising anything absolutely vital. You are just giving your mind the chance to pick up some interesting things that will spice up your exam answers. If you want to prove that you've absorbed something, explain it verbally to a poor relative or friend or spouse.

   TIP: *Don't study from group study papers.* Group study papers – by which I mean summaries of course work prepared by individuals and then shared among a group – are fine at one level but they produce two problems. One is: the point of the distilled notes is that you yourself have put your brain through the mill of the much larger body of knowledge that they summarise. If you just have someone else's notes, THAT'S ALL YOU HAVE. It's a shortcut to disaster. Second, the group study paper leads to everyone writing EXACTLY the same thing. As a marker, there is nothing more tiresome than reading the same study paper – often with the same errors in it – 30 or 40 times in the one session of marking. Study paper answers rarely fail, but they rarely excel, and it is kind of disappointing as an educator to read them.

4. **The night before and the day of the exam.** Return to your A4 sheets. You might have 5 of them. Everything is simple, clear and tidy. Get a good night's sleep – don't pull an all-nighter: that's suicidal. Whatever you do at this stage, DON'T TALK TO OTHER STUDENTS. It will only cause you stress and anxiety. For this reason, I recommend arriving at the exam moments before you are due to walk in to the exam room. Your confidence is precious– if you arrive an hour before, every other bozo will be walking around saying 'did you read up on Moltmann's view of impassability' and you won't have and then you'll get frantic and you'll forget the really important stuff. Believe me.

The key to a theology exam is to remember that it isn't like a maths exam. You only have to write what you know; but you do have to write what you know. There are a number of ways to answer any of the questions. Not remembering Moltmann is (in most cases) completely fine, because you will be able to put other things down instead. Unless there is a question explicitly about Moltmann, but then you'd probably have been told that already...

5. **In the exam room**. Think before you write. Exams take different formats, I know: some stress your ability to think on your feet, some test your recall of material. Most are a combination. The temptation is to settle your nerves by engaging in some frantic writing. Don't. What you need to do right now is put all the info in your head down on paper. There's two strategies here. 1) do all your plans for all the exam essays first. Allow five minutes per question. 2) do your plan for each question as you go. Notice how there isn't a non-planning option? You'll write more if you spend five minutes of your time planning what you'll write. Just go with me here. Shut out the sounds of scribbling all around you.

Actually, you should have planned your time in the exam beforehand. Carefully and accurately divide up the time available between the questions. And plan to stick to the time for each essay pretty rigidly. That's your best mathematical chance for a good result: better three strong essays than one outstanding one and two sketches that score a pass. And use ALL the time you have. It never ceases to amaze me to see students walk out of exams early – I just don't get that at all. I guarantee that the answers those students give aren't as good as they could be because they haven't planned their answers carefully. I don't think they are doing the best that they can do!

As you plan do three things:

a) just put everything you can remember that is relevant down on the paper. Then you won't be anxious about recalling it. Quotes, references, points, whatever.

b) write a thesis statement in response to the question. You are being asked to analyse, synthesis and criticise – not to describe or regurgitate. If the question isn't in the form of an argument MAKE IT INTO ONE. The best answers will always show the capacity for these high order intellectual processes – so find an excuse to show that you can do them. And make sure you are actually answering the question, not simply regurgitating the answer you prepared earlier. It is so obvious when people do that, and try to squash their prepared answer into a question that doesn't quite fit.

c) make a list of points. These points are going to form the body of your essay. Think in this way: 'I am going to argue XYZ. XYZ is true for these reasons'. List them.

6. **Get writing.** Yup, start writing. A couple of things about writing: it is a bit of lost skill, because we type now more often than not. Write legibly in large letters. If you have a problem in this area, leave a clear line in between each written line. Messy writing is often completely readable, but not if it is really, really tiny. As a marker, I can't give you credit for what I can't read. Don't be obsessed about neatness, though: some of the worst exam answers are perfectly neat. There's no time for that! If you make a mistake, don't scribble it out: just make a quick, tidy line through the mistake and move on. Don't waste your time with correction fluid. Like I said: no place

for perfectionists here! Also, we aren't looking for a novelist's prose. Just write directly and efficiently. Say what you mean.

7. **Write a great introduction.** The marker wants to see from the outset that your essay is going to be a) an argument b) an analysis c) well informed. Your intro is your chance to put it all in a nutshell. YOUR FIRST SENTENCE MUST ANSWER THE QUESTION – preferably in the terms of the question. That's not to say you automatically get downgraded for not doing this: I am naming this as a tactic that produces a fine result in clear communication. Then give a potted summary of the things you will talk about. It should be three sentences or perhaps four – not too much detail.

8. **Use numbers to help frame your essay.** It is a good idea to use a numbering system in your paragraphs – it helps you see what you are doing and it makes for very clear communication. One tip though: don't start by nominating a number of points you will make. You may want to add one later on as you think about it.

9. **Use Scripture.** In theology it is simple: no Bible, no pass. Now: don't get hung up on trying to remember lists of proof texts. scriptural evidence can be used in a number of ways (just look at the NT writers!). You can speak generally of the argument of a book: 'In Romans, Paul argues that the gospel is the basis for the justification of the ungodly'. You can name a theme within a book. Or you can pick up a fragment of a verse to quote. If you can't remember chapter and verse, don't worry. Still put it in.

You should also remember to think in terms of the whole canon of Scripture.

1) that means, that you need to consider the Bible as a narrative whole, with Christ at the centre. No Christ = inadequate Christian theology. Where does Jesus/ the gospel fit in?

2) use the whole array of Scripture in your answer. Don't simply answer from Paul – use John, George and Ringo as well. Um, oops – I mean: ask – what is the Johannine take on this? What do the Gospels say? Deuteronomy? the Wisdom literature? Psalms? 1 Peter?

TIP: bone up on John 14–17 and 1 Peter and Hebrews in preparation for your exam. Students tend to know Pauline theology pretty well. But a fully scriptural answer ought to include these perspectives, and these three texts provide some of the richest theological material in the New Testament. From the OT, Isaiah, Deuteronomy and Genesis will be your great helps. And Wisdom literature. Show you know more than one set of texts and you can synthesise their teaching theologically.

10. **Refer to theologians.** Ice your cake by showing that you know that these issues have been discussed down the last two millennia by people with bigger brains than yours. Irenaeus, Augustine, Calvin, Luther, and so on. Now: you don't need to quote them, though quotation is nice. Knowing what they said in your own words is just as good. On the whole, memorising quotes produces stress in your preparation for little value in the exam room. If you do use quotes, make them SHORT. Even four words is fine. 'This man is man' – K. Barth. There's a great quote to use – but know what the author is trying to say by it.

The theologian might be a friend who helps deepen your thoughts and adds authority to your argument, or an enemy against whom you are sparring. Be careful in either case. Your ability to discern shades of grey is more vital here than your rhetorical power in black or white.

11. **Write a simple, one sentence conclusion.** Your conclusion shouldn't waste your time. It is just good form to write a closing sentence that ties everything together. If you have thought of new material on the way through, you could mention it here. If you haven't quite finished your essay and your time for that essay runs out, make a quick list of the extra points you were intending to cover and move on. We can't mark what you don't put down on the paper.

12. **Have a quick re-read.** Don't waste too much time here, but if you can correct some errors, or make some slight additions, you might improve the impression your essay creates.

13. **Emergency measures.** If you are completely thrown by an essay that you haven't prepared for, never mind. You aren't being marked on what you don't know, but only on what you do. So get down on paper as much as you possibly can about the topic. Most theology students have a good Bible knowledge from which they can work anyhow. You'll surprise yourself what your memory and adrenaline can produce. NEVER EVER LEAVE A QUESTION UNANSWERED.

God bless for the exams!

Further reading

Karl Barth *Evangelical Theology: An Introduction* (Grand Rapids: Eerdmans, 1992)

Helmut Thielicke *A Little Exercise for Young Theologians* (Grand Rapids: Eerdmans, 1962)

Anthony Weston *A Rule Book for Arguments* (Indianapolis: Hackett, 2008)

George Orwell, 'Politics and the English Language', https://www.mtholyoke.edu/acad/intrel/orwell46.htm

LATIMER PUBLICATIONS

LATIMER STUDIES

LATIMER PUBLICATIONS

LATIMER PUBLICATIONS

CPSIA information can be obtained
at www.ICGtesting.com
Printed in the USA
LVHW091541130619
621125LV00001B/230/P

9 781906 327125